SQL Mastery
Unlock the Power of Databases and Queries

A Comprehensive Guide to Mastering SQL for Developers

MIGUEL FARMER

RAFAEL SANDER

Table of Content

TABLE OF CONTENTS

INTRODUCTION

SQL Mastery: Unlock the Power of Databases and Queries

In the fast-paced world of software development, understanding **SQL** (Structured Query Language) is not just beneficial—it's essential. Whether you're a seasoned developer, a database administrator, or someone just starting your career in the tech industry, mastering SQL can empower you to interact with and manage the backbone of modern applications: **databases**.

This book, **"SQL Mastery: Unlock the Power of Databases and Queries"**, is designed to help you do exactly that—unlock the potential of SQL and become a true SQL master. It offers a **comprehensive guide** to SQL, from the foundational concepts to advanced techniques, with **real-world examples** to guide you through practical applications of SQL in modern development environments.

Why This Book is Essential for Developers

SQL has stood the test of time for over four decades, and its importance has only grown as the world becomes more data-driven. **Relational databases**—powered by SQL—are still at the core of countless applications, ranging from financial systems to social media platforms. If you are building an **enterprise application**, working with **big data**, or managing a **cloud-based system**, SQL is likely the primary language you'll use to manage, query, and retrieve data.

However, with the increasing complexity of applications and the rise of new technologies such as **NoSQL, big data**, and **cloud computing**, understanding how to effectively leverage SQL has become more crucial than ever. This book provides not only an in-depth introduction to SQL but also covers how SQL interacts with modern technologies like **NoSQL databases, cloud solutions**, and **real-time data processing**, offering you the skills needed to work in today's complex development environments.

What You Will Learn in This Book

1. Building a Strong Foundation in SQL

This book starts with the basics of **SQL syntax, data types**, and **table design**. Whether you're a complete beginner or have some prior experience, the early chapters provide clear, step-by-step explanations to get you up and running. You will learn how to create and manage tables, insert and update data, and execute basic queries. **Joins, subqueries**, and **aggregations** will become second nature as we explore SQL's power in querying relational data.

2. Mastering Complex Queries

As you progress, you will dive deeper into more advanced SQL techniques. This includes the powerful **Common Table Expressions (CTEs)** and **recursive queries**, which allow you to handle hierarchical data and simplify complex queries. We'll explore **window functions** to perform running totals, rankings, and analytics—tools essential for performing advanced calculations without compromising performance.

3. Database Optimization and Performance Tuning

SQL is not just about writing queries; it's also about writing **efficient** queries. In later chapters, we will examine **performance optimization** techniques, including **indexing**, **query optimization**, and **caching** strategies. You will learn how to structure your queries and design databases that scale well as data volume grows. The ability to **optimize database performance** is a skill that every developer and database administrator needs to master.

4. Advanced SQL Techniques

For those who wish to go beyond the basics, this book introduces advanced concepts like **stored procedures**, **triggers**, **user-defined functions**, and **transactions**. These concepts are key to building sophisticated applications that can perform complex operations efficiently. We also explore **advanced joins**, **subqueries**, and **data integrity techniques**, providing you with the tools to handle even the most complex relational data models.

5. Real-World Applications and Modern Tools

One of the highlights of this book is its focus on **real-world examples**. Each chapter includes practical scenarios to help you understand how to use SQL in real-life applications. For instance, we explore how to build and query a **sales reporting system**, how to handle **big data** in SQL databases, and how to implement **real-time analytics**. As we move forward, we also touch on new technologies, such as **cloud databases**, **SQL on big data platforms**, and **NoSQL integrations**, ensuring you are prepared for the future of data management.

For Whom Is This Book Intended?

This book is written for:

- **Beginner and Intermediate SQL Learners**: If you're new to SQL or have some experience but want to deepen your knowledge, this book is perfect for you. We cover the fundamentals, gradually advancing to more complex topics.

- **Experienced Developers and Database Administrators**: Even for those with years of experience in the field, this book will challenge you with advanced techniques and provide insights into **modern tools and frameworks** that are shaping the future of SQL databases.

- **Data Enthusiasts and Engineers**: Anyone working with large-scale databases, cloud databases, or **big data platforms** will benefit from understanding how SQL fits into the broader landscape of modern database technology.

What Makes This Book Different?

While many books cover SQL, **"SQL Mastery"** takes a **holistic approach** by not only teaching you SQL syntax but also ensuring you understand how SQL fits into modern data architectures and development practices. We address:

- **SQL in the age of cloud computing** and how to work with cloud databases like **AWS RDS, Google Cloud SQL**, and **Azure SQL**.
- The rise of **NoSQL** and how SQL can still coexist with non-relational databases.
- **Real-time analytics** and **data streaming**, which are becoming crucial in data-intensive applications.

Moreover, this book is **jargon-free**, ensuring that complex topics are explained in a straightforward manner with **real-world examples** to help you grasp the concepts quickly.

Real-World Focus: Building Practical Solutions

Each chapter comes with **practical examples** drawn from real-world scenarios, helping you bridge the gap between theory and practice. By the end of the book, you'll be able to:

- Design and manage complex relational databases.
- Optimize SQL queries for performance and scalability.
- Build and maintain databases that power modern applications, from e-commerce platforms to real-time data analytics.

- Work with SQL in cloud environments and hybrid systems, preparing you for the future of database management.

Conclusion

SQL Mastery: Unlock the Power of Databases and Queries is not just a guide to learning SQL—it's a comprehensive roadmap to becoming a **SQL expert**. Whether you are a beginner or an experienced professional, this book will provide you with the tools, techniques, and knowledge you need to **master SQL** and take your data management skills to the next level.

Let's dive into the world of SQL and discover how this essential language can transform your ability to manage and query data, optimize performance, and build powerful, scalable applications.

CHAPTER 1

INTRODUCTION TO SQL AND DATABASES

In the world of software development, databases play a central role in storing, managing, and retrieving data. Whether you're working on a small personal project or a large enterprise system, the ability to interact with data efficiently and effectively is key to building powerful applications. One of the most important tools for interacting with databases is **SQL (Structured Query Language)**.

In this chapter, we will explore the basics of SQL and relational databases, and why mastering SQL is an essential skill for developers. By the end of this chapter, you'll understand the importance of SQL, its core concepts, and how it powers modern applications.

What is SQL?

SQL, or **Structured Query Language**, is a programming language used to manage and manipulate data stored in **relational databases**. It allows you to perform tasks like querying data,

15

inserting new data, updating existing records, and deleting data, all in a structured and consistent manner.

SQL is both **simple** and **powerful**—you don't need to write complex code to interact with databases, but you can still accomplish complex operations with just a few lines of SQL.

Key SQL Operations:

1. **SELECT** – Retrieves data from a database.
2. **INSERT** – Adds new data to a database.
3. **UPDATE** – Modifies existing data in a database.
4. **DELETE** – Removes data from a database.
5. **CREATE** – Defines new database structures (e.g., tables).
6. **ALTER** – Modifies an existing database structure.
7. **DROP** – Deletes database objects like tables or views.

SQL Syntax:

SQL statements are written using a specific syntax, but the language itself is relatively straightforward. Here's an example of a basic query:

```sql
SELECT name, age FROM employees WHERE department = 'Sales';
```

In this query:

- **SELECT** is used to fetch data.
- **name, age** are the columns we want to retrieve.
- **FROM employees** specifies the table where the data is stored.
- **WHERE department = 'Sales'** filters the data to only return employees in the Sales department.

SQL's simplicity and readability make it an essential tool for developers, enabling them to quickly retrieve and manipulate data stored in relational databases.

Relational Databases: Core Concepts

Relational databases are the foundation of SQL. A **relational database** is a type of database that stores data in **tables**. Each table is made up of rows and columns, with each row representing a single record and each column representing a property or attribute of that record.

Here are the core concepts behind relational databases:

1. Tables

A table is the basic structure used to store data in a relational database. A table consists of rows and columns. Each row represents a **record**, while each column represents an **attribute** of the record.

Example of a simple **Employee** table:

ID	Name	Department	Age
1	John Doe	Sales	32
2	Jane Smith	HR	28
3	Alice Brown	IT	40

2. Primary Keys

A **primary key** is a unique identifier for a record within a table. It ensures that each row in the table can be uniquely identified. For example, in the **Employee** table, the **ID** column can be the primary key.

3. Foreign Keys

A **foreign key** is a column or set of columns in one table that links to the primary key of another table. This relationship between tables is what makes databases "relational." Foreign keys help enforce data integrity by ensuring that the relationship between tables is valid.

For example, in an **Order** table, you might have a foreign key linking to the **Employee** table to represent which employee took the order.

4. Relationships

Relational databases allow for relationships between tables, such as:

- **One-to-One**: Each record in one table corresponds to one record in another table (e.g., one employee has one employee ID).
- **One-to-Many**: Each record in one table corresponds to many records in another table (e.g., one department has many employees).
- **Many-to-Many**: Multiple records in one table correspond to multiple records in another table (e.g., students enrolled in multiple courses, and each course has multiple students).

Why SQL is Essential for Developers

SQL is an essential skill for developers, especially those working with **relational databases**, as it directly impacts their ability to interact with and manipulate data. Here's why SQL is so important:

19

1. Data Retrieval

SQL enables developers to easily **retrieve** data from databases using **queries**. Whether it's pulling a list of all users, filtering products by price, or aggregating sales data, SQL gives you the power to quickly and efficiently get the data you need.

2. Data Manipulation

SQL is used for **inserting**, **updating**, and **deleting** data in databases. For example, you might insert a new customer into a database, update a product's price, or remove an order record that was mistakenly created.

3. Database Design

As a developer, you'll often work with **database schemas**—the structure of your database, including tables, columns, and relationships. SQL is used to **define** and **alter** these structures to match the evolving needs of the application.

4. Scalability

With SQL, you can design **scalable databases** that can handle large amounts of data and growing applications. By using **indexes**, **views**, and **stored procedures**, you can ensure that your database performs well even as your application grows.

5. Performance Tuning

SQL allows you to optimize queries for faster performance, helping you avoid bottlenecks in data access. By understanding how to use **joins**, **subqueries**, **grouping**, and **indexes** effectively, you can optimize your database operations and improve the speed of your application.

6. Interoperability

SQL is a **universal language** for relational databases. Whether you're working with **MySQL**, **PostgreSQL**, **SQL Server**, or **SQLite**, the basic SQL syntax remains consistent across platforms. This makes it easier to migrate between different databases and ensures that your skills are transferable across different projects and organizations.

Real-World Examples: How SQL Powers Modern Applications

SQL is not just a tool used by database administrators; it is an essential skill for developers working on modern applications. Let's look at how SQL is used in real-world scenarios:

1. E-commerce Platforms

In an e-commerce application, SQL is used to store and manage data related to customers, products, orders, inventory, and payments. Here's how SQL is involved in an e-commerce system:

- Retrieving a list of products based on user preferences (e.g., filtering products by category, price range, or brand).
- Storing and retrieving customer data, including order history and payment information.
- Managing inventory and ensuring that stock levels are updated after each purchase.

Example Query: **Get all products in the 'Electronics' category priced between $100 and $500.**

sql

```
SELECT product_name, price, category
FROM products
WHERE category = 'Electronics' AND price BETWEEN
100 AND 500;
```

2. Social Media Applications

In social media platforms, SQL is used to manage user data, posts, comments, likes, and interactions. SQL queries can help:

- Retrieve a user's posts and comments.
- Update a user's profile information.
- Query the number of likes or shares a post has received.

Example Query: **Get the posts made by a specific user and the number of comments on each post.**

sql

```
SELECT          posts.post_id,          posts.content,
COUNT(comments.comment_id) AS comment_count
FROM posts
LEFT    JOIN    comments    ON    posts.post_id    =
comments.post_id
WHERE posts.user_id = 1
GROUP BY posts.post_id;
```

3. Banking and Financial Applications

SQL is crucial for managing transactions in **banking systems**. This includes:

- Storing user account information (balance, account type, etc.).
- Tracking deposits, withdrawals, and transfers.
- Calculating interest and generating reports.

Example Query: **Get the transaction history for a specific bank account.**

23

```sql
sql


SELECT transaction_id, transaction_type, amount, date
FROM transactions
WHERE account_id = 12345
ORDER BY date DESC;
```

Conclusion

In this chapter, we've explored the **fundamentals of SQL** and its role in database management. We learned how SQL is used to interact with **relational databases**, covering basic SQL operations like SELECT, INSERT, UPDATE, DELETE, and more. We also discussed why SQL is an essential tool for developers, enabling them to retrieve, manipulate, and store data efficiently.

As you progress through this book, you will build on these concepts, learning how to handle more advanced database operations, optimize queries for performance, and apply real-world use cases to build robust, scalable applications.

Feel free to move forward to the next chapter, where we'll dive deeper into setting up your **SQL environment** and start writing more advanced queries!

CHAPTER 2

SETTING UP YOUR SQL ENVIRONMENT

Before diving deep into SQL and its practical applications, it's essential to get your development environment set up properly. Whether you're working with **MySQL**, **PostgreSQL**, or **SQLite**, each of these database management systems (DBMS) has its own setup process and tools. In this chapter, we will guide you through the process of **installing** and **configuring** MySQL, PostgreSQL, and SQLite, setting up **SQL clients** and **IDEs** (Integrated Development Environments), and show you how to use these tools effectively for your SQL development.

Installing and Configuring MySQL, PostgreSQL, or SQLite

Let's walk through the setup and installation process for the three most commonly used relational databases: **MySQL**, **PostgreSQL**, and **SQLite**. These databases will serve as the foundation for the queries and operations you will learn throughout this book.

1. Installing MySQL

MySQL is one of the most popular and widely used relational database management systems. It is known for its speed, reliability, and ease of use, making it a great choice for developers.

Installation on Windows:

1. Download the MySQL installer from the official website: MySQL Downloads.
2. Run the installer and choose **MySQL Server**.
3. Follow the installation steps and select the **Developer Default** setup, which includes MySQL Server and other necessary components.
4. Set the root password and configure other settings.
5. Once installation is complete, you can start MySQL through the **MySQL Workbench** or from the command line.

Installation on macOS:

1. You can install MySQL using **Homebrew**, a package manager for macOS:

bash

```
brew install mysql
```

2. Start MySQL service:

```bash

brew services start mysql
```

3. Secure the installation:

```bash

mysql_secure_installation
```

Installation on Linux (Ubuntu):

1. Install MySQL using apt:

```bash

sudo apt update
sudo apt install mysql-server
```

2. Secure the installation:

```bash

sudo mysql_secure_installation
```

After MySQL is installed, you can access the database by running:

```bash
```

```
mysql -u root -p
```

2. Installing PostgreSQL

PostgreSQL is another powerful relational database, known for its advanced features, scalability, and SQL compliance. It is used in both small and large-scale applications.

Installation on Windows:

1. Download the installer from PostgreSQL Downloads.
2. Run the installer and follow the on-screen instructions.
3. Choose a directory for installation and set the password for the `postgres` superuser.
4. Once installed, you can access the PostgreSQL command line tool (`psql`) to interact with the database.

Installation on macOS:

1. You can use **Homebrew** to install PostgreSQL:

    bash

    ```
    brew install postgresql
    ```

2. Start PostgreSQL service:

    bash

29

```
brew services start postgresql
```

3. Create a new PostgreSQL database:

```
bash
```

```
createdb mydb
```

Installation on Linux (Ubuntu):

1. Install PostgreSQL using apt:

```
bash
```

```
sudo apt update
sudo apt install postgresql postgresql-
contrib
```

2. Switch to the `postgres` user:

```
bash
```

```
sudo -i -u postgres
```

3. Access PostgreSQL:

```
bash
```

```
psql
```

You can now begin working with PostgreSQL from the command line using `psql`.

---

3. Installing SQLite

SQLite is a self-contained, serverless, and zero-configuration SQL database engine. It's commonly used for smaller applications, local databases, or in development environments. Its simplicity makes it an ideal choice for **prototyping** or **testing**.

Installation on Windows:

1. Download the precompiled binaries from SQLite Downloads.
2. Extract the ZIP file to a directory of your choice.
3. Add the SQLite directory to your system's PATH environment variable so you can use SQLite from the command line.

Installation on macOS:

1. SQLite comes pre-installed on most macOS versions. You can check by running:

```bash
sqlite3 --version
```

2. If it's not installed, you can use **Homebrew**:

```bash
```

```bash
brew install sqlite
```

Installation on Linux (Ubuntu):

1. Install SQLite using apt:

```bash
```

```bash
sudo apt update
sudo apt install sqlite3
```

To use SQLite, simply create or open a database file using the sqlite3 command:

```bash
```

```bash
sqlite3 mydatabase.db
```

Working with Database Management Systems (DBMS)

Once you've installed the database management system of your choice, it's time to interact with it. Here's a breakdown of how to work with these DBMS:

1. MySQL Workbench (For MySQL)

MySQL Workbench is a popular tool for managing MySQL databases. It provides a graphical interface for creating databases, writing queries, and managing users and permissions.

- **Launching MySQL Workbench**: After installation, you can launch MySQL Workbench and connect to the MySQL server by providing your `root` password.
- **Running Queries**: You can open the query editor, write your SQL queries, and execute them directly from the interface.

2. pgAdmin (For PostgreSQL)

pgAdmin is a feature-rich administration tool for PostgreSQL. It allows you to manage databases, execute queries, and visualize database structures.

- **Launching pgAdmin**: After installation, launch pgAdmin, and connect to your PostgreSQL server by providing the `postgres` user password.
- **Creating Databases and Tables**: You can create new databases, tables, and run SQL queries from the SQL Query Tool.

3. SQLite Command Line (For SQLite)

SQLite doesn't require a server, and you interact with it directly using the command line interface.

- **Creating a Database**: You can create a new database by simply running `sqlite3 mydatabase.db`.
- **Running Queries**: You can write and execute SQL commands directly in the interactive shell.

Using SQL Clients and IDEs

Many developers prefer using **SQL clients** and **IDEs** (Integrated Development Environments) for easier database management and query execution. Some of the most popular tools for interacting with SQL databases include:

1. DBeaver

DBeaver is a universal database management tool that supports MySQL, PostgreSQL, SQLite, and other databases. It provides an easy-to-use interface for running queries, managing database structures, and performing administrative tasks.

2. DataGrip

DataGrip, from JetBrains, is a powerful IDE for SQL development. It supports multiple databases and provides advanced features like code completion, query formatting, and database visualization.

3. SQL Server Management Studio (SSMS)

SSMS is the official IDE for managing Microsoft SQL Server databases. It provides tools for query execution, performance tuning, and data management.

4. HeidiSQL

HeidiSQL is a lightweight SQL client for MySQL and MariaDB databases. It's simple, yet powerful, allowing you to easily manage databases, write queries, and edit data.

Real-World Example: Setting Up a Local Database for Development

Let's walk through setting up a **local MySQL database** for a **development environment**.

1. Install MySQL Server:

Follow the installation steps from earlier in this chapter to set up MySQL on your machine.

2. Create a New Database:

Once MySQL is running, log into the MySQL shell:

bash

```
mysql -u root -p
```

Create a new database for your project:

sql

```
CREATE DATABASE my_project_db;
```

3. Create a Table:

Let's create a simple users table with id, name, and email columns:

sql

```
USE my_project_db;

CREATE TABLE users (
    id INT AUTO_INCREMENT PRIMARY KEY,
```

```
    name VARCHAR(100),
    email VARCHAR(100)
);
```

4. Insert Sample Data:

Insert some sample data into the `users` table:

sql

```
INSERT INTO users (name, email) VALUES
('Alice', 'alice@example.com'),
('Bob', 'bob@example.com');
```

5. Query the Data:

Now you can query the data from the `users` table:

sql

```
SELECT * FROM users;
```

Conclusion

In this chapter, we have:

- Installed and configured **MySQL**, **PostgreSQL**, and **SQLite**, three of the most commonly used relational database management systems.

37

- Explored how to interact with these DBMS through **SQL clients** and **IDEs**.
- Set up a local database for development, which is an essential step for working with SQL in real-world projects.

As you continue your journey through SQL, you'll be able to leverage these tools to create and manage databases, run queries, and build data-driven applications with confidence.

In the next chapter, we'll dive into **basic SQL syntax and queries**, where we'll start writing queries to retrieve and manipulate data in your database!

CHAPTER 3

UNDERSTANDING RELATIONAL DATABASE DESIGN

When building applications, particularly those involving large amounts of structured data, understanding **relational database design** is essential. The way data is structured in a relational database plays a significant role in the efficiency, scalability, and performance of your application. In this chapter, we'll dive deep into the concepts of **tables**, **rows**, and **columns**, and explore key database concepts like **primary keys**, **foreign keys**, **constraints**, **normalization**, and **denormalization**. By the end of this chapter, you'll have a strong foundation in database design that will help you build more efficient and maintainable data models.

Tables, Rows, and Columns

The foundation of any relational database is the **table**, where data is stored in a structured manner. A table consists of **rows** and **columns**, each of which plays a specific role in how data is organized and accessed.

1. Tables

A **table** is a collection of related data organized into rows and columns. Each table typically represents an entity in your application, such as **users**, **products**, **orders**, etc.

- **Example**: A table for **products** in an e-commerce store might include information like the product name, description, price, and stock quantity.

2. Rows

Each **row** represents a single record or instance of the entity represented by the table. For example, in the **products** table, each row would represent a single product.

- **Example**: A row in the **products** table might represent a product like "Wireless Mouse" with specific details (name, description, price).

3. Columns

Columns represent attributes or properties of the entity. Each column holds a specific type of data (e.g., strings, integers, dates) and defines what kind of information each row will contain.

- **Example**: In the **products** table, columns could include product_name, description, price, stock_quantity, etc.

Visual Representation:

Let's take a look at a table structure:

product_id	product_name	description	price	stock_quantity
1	Wireless Mouse	A smooth mouse	29.99	150
2	Gaming Keyboard	RGB mechanical keys	99.99	80

- The **product_id** is the unique identifier for each product.
- **product_name, description, price**, and **stock_quantity** are the columns that hold the attributes of each product.

Primary Keys, Foreign Keys, and Constraints

When designing a relational database, ensuring data integrity and consistency is essential. This is where **primary keys**, **foreign keys**, and **constraints** come in.

41

1. Primary Keys

A **primary key** uniquely identifies each record in a table. It must contain unique values and cannot contain NULL values. The primary key ensures that each record is distinct from all others.

- **Example**: In the **products** table, product_id might be the primary key because it uniquely identifies each product.

Primary Key Rules:

- Must be unique for every row.
- Cannot contain NULL values.

2. Foreign Keys

A **foreign key** is a column (or set of columns) in one table that links to the **primary key** in another table. Foreign keys create relationships between tables and enforce referential integrity, ensuring that data in one table corresponds to valid data in another.

- **Example**: In an **orders** table, you might have a user_id column that references the user_id in the **users** table, linking each order to a specific user.

Foreign Key Rules:

- The foreign key must match a valid primary key in the referenced table.
- Foreign keys enforce relationships between tables, ensuring data consistency.

3. Constraints

Constraints are rules that restrict the type of data that can be inserted or updated in a table. Constraints can be used to enforce data integrity and ensure that the data meets certain conditions.

Common types of constraints:

- **NOT NULL**: Ensures that a column cannot contain NULL values.
- **UNIQUE**: Ensures that all values in a column are unique.
- **CHECK**: Ensures that values in a column meet a specified condition.
- **DEFAULT**: Provides a default value for a column if no value is provided.

Example: In the **orders** table, you could use a constraint to ensure that the **order_amount** column cannot be negative:

sql

```
ALTER TABLE orders ADD CONSTRAINT
check_order_amount CHECK (order_amount >= 0);
```

Normalization and Denormalization

1. Normalization

Normalization is the process of organizing data in a database to reduce redundancy and dependency by dividing large tables into smaller, related tables. The goal of normalization is to ensure that each piece of data is stored only once, reducing data duplication and improving data integrity.

There are several normal forms, each with specific rules:

- **First Normal Form (1NF)**: Ensures that each column contains atomic values (no multiple values in a single column).
- **Second Normal Form (2NF)**: Ensures that all non-key attributes are fully dependent on the primary key.
- **Third Normal Form (3NF)**: Ensures that there are no transitive dependencies (i.e., non-key columns shouldn't depend on other non-key columns).

Example: Let's say we have a `students_courses` table that stores information about students and the courses they are enrolled in:

student_id	student_name	course_name	course_instructor
1	John Doe	Math 101	Dr. Smith
1	John Doe	Physics 101	Dr. Johnson

This table contains **redundant data** (John Doe's name and course details appear multiple times). To normalize this, we can break the table into two:

1. **Students Table**:

student_id	student_name
1	John Doe

2. **Courses Table**:

course_id	course_name	course_instructor
101	Math 101	Dr. Smith
102	Physics 101	Dr. Johnson

3. **Enrollments Table** (a relationship table between students and courses):

student_id	course_id
1	101
1	102

This process ensures that data is more organized and that redundancies are minimized.

2. Denormalization

Denormalization is the opposite of normalization. It involves intentionally introducing some redundancy into a database design for the sake of performance. This is typically done to **speed up read operations**, especially when data retrieval is more critical than data storage efficiency.

While **normalized databases** are efficient for handling complex queries and large amounts of data with minimal redundancy, **denormalized databases** can be used to speed up queries that involve **joining multiple tables** or retrieving aggregated data.

Example: In a **denormalized e-commerce database**, you might store both **user information** and **order details** in the same table, even though this would result in data duplication, to improve the speed of queries that return all order-related data in one go.

Real-World Example: Designing a Database for an E-commerce Application

Let's design a basic **database** for an **e-commerce application**. The application will involve customers, orders, products, and payments.

Step 1: Identify the Core Entities

In an e-commerce system, the core entities are:

- **Customers** (who are buying products)
- **Products** (items being sold)
- **Orders** (representing purchases made by customers)
- **Payments** (records of transactions made by customers)

Step 2: Design the Tables

We need tables for each of these entities, along with the relationships between them.

1. **Customers Table:**

customer_id	first_name	last_name	email	phone_number
1	Alice	Johnson	alice@email.com	1234567890

2. **Products Table**:

product_id	product_name	description	price	stock_quantity
1	Laptop	15-inch screen	999.99	50

3. **Orders Table**:

order_id	customer_id	order_date	order_total
1	1	2023-10-05	999.99

4. **Order_Items Table** (Relationship between orders and products):

order_id	product_id	quantity	price_per_item
1	1	1	999.99

5. **Payments Table**:

payment_id	order_id	payment_date	payment_method	amount_paid
1	1	2023-10-05	Credit Card	999.99

Step 3: Define Relationships

- A **customer** can place multiple **orders** (one-to-many).
- Each **order** can contain multiple **products** (many-to-many, implemented via `Order_Items`).
- An **order** can have one **payment** (one-to-one).

Conclusion

In this chapter, we covered the essential concepts of **relational database design**, focusing on the core structures (tables, rows, and columns), how to establish relationships between data using **primary keys** and **foreign keys**, and the importance of **normalization** and **denormalization** for maintaining data integrity and performance.

We also explored a **real-world example** of designing a database for an **e-commerce application**, which reinforced the concepts learned and helped us apply them to a practical scenario.

With a solid understanding of relational database design, you're now ready to start creating your own databases for real-world applications. In the next chapter, we will begin writing SQL queries to retrieve and manipulate data in these databases!

CHAPTER 4

BASIC SQL SYNTAX AND QUERIES

SQL, or **Structured Query Language**, is used to interact with relational databases. In this chapter, we'll focus on the basics of writing SQL queries, specifically **SELECT statements** for retrieving data from a table, using the **WHERE clause** for filtering data, and **sorting and limiting results**. These are the most fundamental SQL operations you'll use every day when working with databases.

We will also walk through a **real-world example** of querying customer information in a **Customer Relationship Management (CRM)** database to reinforce these concepts.

1. SELECT Statements: Retrieving Data from a Table

The most basic operation in SQL is retrieving data from a table. This is done using the **SELECT** statement.

The **SELECT** statement allows you to specify the columns you want to retrieve from a table, and it's the first step in querying data from a database.

Basic SELECT Syntax:

sql

```
SELECT column1, column2, column3
FROM table_name;
```

- `column1, column2, column3`: The specific columns you want to retrieve from the table.
- `table_name`: The name of the table from which to retrieve the data.

Example: Retrieving All Data from a Table

Suppose we have a `customers` table with the following columns: `customer_id`, `first_name`, `last_name`, `email`, and `phone_number`. To retrieve all customer information from the table, we would use the following query:

sql

```
SELECT * FROM customers;
```

- The `*` symbol means "all columns." This query retrieves all data from the `customers` table.

Example Output:

customer_id	first_name	last_name	email	phone_number
1	Alice	Johnson	alice@email.com	1234567890
2	Bob	Smith	bob@email.com	9876543210

2. Using WHERE Clauses for Filtering

The **WHERE** clause allows you to filter records based on specific conditions. This is one of the most commonly used SQL operations. With **WHERE**, you can restrict the data that is retrieved by applying filters on the data.

Basic WHERE Syntax:

sql

```
SELECT column1, column2
FROM table_name
WHERE condition;
```

- condition: The condition that must be true for the row to be included in the results (e.g., column1 = 'value').

Common Operators in WHERE Clauses:

- =: Equals
- != or <>: Not equal to
- >: Greater than
- <: Less than
- >=: Greater than or equal to
- <=: Less than or equal to
- BETWEEN: Range of values (e.g., between two dates)
- IN: A list of values
- LIKE: Pattern matching (e.g., for partial matches)
- IS NULL: Checking for null values

Example: Filtering with WHERE Clause

Let's say we want to retrieve information about customers who live in the "Sales" department. Assuming there is a department column in the customers table, the query would be:

sql

```
SELECT * FROM customers
WHERE department = 'Sales';
```

This query will return all customers whose department is "Sales."

Example with Numerical Condition

To retrieve all customers whose `customer_id` is greater than 100:

sql

```
SELECT * FROM customers
WHERE customer_id > 100;
```

---

3. Sorting and Limiting Results

In addition to filtering data with the **WHERE** clause, you may also want to sort the results or limit the number of rows returned.

3.1. Sorting Results with ORDER BY

You can use the **ORDER BY** clause to sort the result set in ascending or descending order.

Basic ORDER BY Syntax:

sql

```
SELECT column1, column2
FROM table_name
ORDER BY column1 [ASC | DESC];
```

- `ASC`: Sorts in ascending order (this is the default).

- DESC: Sorts in descending order.

Example: Sorting Results by Last Name

If we want to sort customers by their last name in **ascending order**:

sql

```
SELECT * FROM customers
ORDER BY last_name ASC;
```

To sort the results by last_name in **descending order**:

sql

```
SELECT * FROM customers
ORDER BY last_name DESC;
```

3.2. Limiting the Number of Rows

You can use the **LIMIT** clause to restrict the number of rows returned by the query.

Basic LIMIT Syntax:

sql

```
SELECT column1, column2
FROM table_name
LIMIT number_of_rows;
```

- `number_of_rows`: The maximum number of rows to return.

Example: Retrieving Only the First 5 Customers

To retrieve only the first 5 customers from the table:

```sql
SELECT * FROM customers
LIMIT 5;
```

This query will return the first 5 records from the `customers` table.

Real-World Example: Querying Customer Information in a CRM Database

Let's walk through a real-world example where we query customer information in a **Customer Relationship Management (CRM)** system. We'll apply the SQL skills we've learned so far to perform various operations, such as retrieving customer details, filtering by certain conditions, and sorting the data.

Example 1: Retrieving All Customer Information

We want to get a list of all customers in our CRM system:

57

sql

```
SELECT * FROM customers;
```

This will retrieve every column for every customer in the database.

Example 2: Retrieving Customer Emails for a Specific Department

Now, let's say we want to retrieve the emails of customers in the "Marketing" department:

sql

```
SELECT email FROM customers
WHERE department = 'Marketing';
```

This query will return only the email addresses of customers in the Marketing department.

Example 3: Retrieving Customers Who Joined After a Specific Date

If we have a `join_date` column, and we want to find all customers who joined after January 1, 2020, we can use the BETWEEN operator:

sql

```
SELECT first_name, last_name, join_date
```

```
FROM customers
WHERE join_date BETWEEN '2020-01-01' AND '2023-
01-01';
```

This will return all customers who joined between January 1, 2020, and January 1, 2023.

Example 4: Sorting Customers by Last Name in Descending Order

To retrieve a list of customers sorted by their last name, in descending order:

```
sql
```

```
SELECT first_name, last_name
FROM customers
ORDER BY last_name DESC;
```

This will return the customer names in reverse alphabetical order based on their last name.

Example 5: Limiting the Results to the First 10 Customers

If we want to retrieve only the first 10 customers, we can limit the result set:

```
sql
```

```
SELECT * FROM customers
LIMIT 10;
```

This will return only the first 10 records from the `customers` table.

Conclusion

In this chapter, we've covered the basics of **SQL queries**, including:

- The **SELECT statement** for retrieving data from a table.
- The **WHERE clause** for filtering data based on specific conditions.
- Sorting data with **ORDER BY** and limiting results with **LIMIT**.

Through the **real-world example** of querying customer information in a CRM database, you've seen how these fundamental SQL operations can be used in everyday development tasks. These skills form the foundation for working with databases, and as you move forward, you'll learn more advanced SQL techniques to manipulate and analyze your data.

In the next chapter, we'll dive deeper into **aggregating data** using functions like **COUNT, SUM, AVG**, and **GROUP BY** to summarize and analyze data.

CHAPTER 5

FILTERING DATA WITH WHERE CLAUSES

The **WHERE clause** is one of the most important components in SQL for retrieving data that meets specific conditions. It allows you to filter results and narrow down the dataset to match your needs. In this chapter, we'll explore how to use **comparison operators**, **logical operators**, and other advanced filtering techniques like **IN, BETWEEN, LIKE**, and **IS NULL**. We will also look at how to combine multiple conditions to refine queries. We'll end with a **real-world example** of querying orders in a **sales system** to showcase these techniques.

1. Comparison Operators and Logical Operators

Comparison operators allow you to filter rows based on specific conditions. Logical operators allow you to combine multiple conditions to form more complex queries.

Comparison Operators

Comparison operators are used to compare values in SQL. These operators help you filter data based on numeric, string, or date comparisons.

- =: Equal to
- != or <>: Not equal to
- >: Greater than
- <: Less than
- >=: Greater than or equal to
- <=: Less than or equal to

Logical Operators

Logical operators allow you to combine multiple conditions in a query. The most common logical operators are:

- AND: Combines two conditions, and both must be true for a row to be included.
- OR: Combines two conditions, and at least one must be true for a row to be included.
- NOT: Reverses the result of a condition (e.g., NOT LIKE or NOT IN).

Example: Using Comparison Operators

If we want to query all products that cost more than $50, we would write the following SQL query:

sql

```
SELECT * FROM products
WHERE price > 50;
```

To filter orders that are less than $100 or greater than $500:

sql

```
SELECT * FROM orders
WHERE order_total < 100 OR order_total > 500;
```

This query retrieves orders that either have a total less than $100 or greater than $500.

Example: Using AND and OR

To retrieve products that are priced between $100 and $500, we would combine AND:

sql

```
SELECT * FROM products
WHERE price >= 100 AND price <= 500;
```

To retrieve products that are either in the "Electronics" category or priced over $500, use OR:

```sql
sql

SELECT * FROM products
WHERE category = 'Electronics' OR price > 500;
```

---

2. Using IN, BETWEEN, LIKE, and IS NULL

SQL provides more advanced operators that let you filter data in specific ways:

IN Operator

The IN operator allows you to specify multiple values for a column. This is useful when you want to filter rows where a column matches any value in a specified list.

Example: Retrieving products in specific categories

```sql
sql

SELECT * FROM products
WHERE category IN ('Electronics', 'Furniture',
'Clothing');
```

This query retrieves products that belong to any of the categories: "Electronics", "Furniture", or "Clothing".

BETWEEN Operator

The BETWEEN operator is used to filter data based on a range of values, such as numbers, dates, or strings. It is inclusive, meaning it includes the boundary values.

Example: Filtering orders made in a specific date range

sql

```
SELECT * FROM orders
WHERE order_date BETWEEN '2023-01-01' AND '2023-
12-31';
```

This retrieves all orders placed in the year 2023.

LIKE Operator

The LIKE operator is used to search for a specified pattern in a column. It's commonly used for **string matching** and supports the use of wildcard characters:

- % represents zero or more characters.
- _ represents a single character.

Example: Searching for products with names starting with 'L'

65

sql

```
SELECT * FROM products
WHERE product_name LIKE 'L%';
```

This query retrieves products whose names start with the letter "L".

To find customer names that contain "john":

sql

```
SELECT * FROM customers
WHERE first_name LIKE '%john%';
```

IS NULL Operator

The IS NULL operator is used to check if a column contains NULL values. This is particularly useful when you want to find records that have missing or unknown values.

Example: Retrieving customers without an email address

sql

```
SELECT * FROM customers
WHERE email IS NULL;
```

This query retrieves customers whose email address is missing (NULL).

3. Combining Multiple Conditions

You can combine multiple conditions using the logical operators (AND, OR, NOT) to build more complex queries. These operators help you refine your search and narrow down the results even further.

Example: Retrieving products in the 'Electronics' category priced between $100 and $500

sql

```
SELECT * FROM products
WHERE category = 'Electronics'
AND price BETWEEN 100 AND 500;
```

This query retrieves all products in the "Electronics" category whose price is between $100 and $500.

Example: Retrieving orders placed by customers from 'New York' or 'Los Angeles'

sql

```
SELECT * FROM orders
WHERE customer_id IN (SELECT customer_id FROM
customers WHERE city IN ('New York', 'Los
Angeles'));
```

This query retrieves orders placed by customers who are from either New York or Los Angeles.

Example: Excluding Records Using NOT

If you want to exclude a specific value, use the NOT operator.

sql

```
SELECT * FROM products
WHERE category NOT IN ('Furniture', 'Clothing');
```

This query retrieves all products except those in the "Furniture" or "Clothing" categories.

Real-World Example: Querying Orders in a Sales System

Let's put all these filtering techniques into practice with a real-world example. Suppose we have a **Sales System** that tracks orders made by customers. The **orders** table includes columns like order_id, order_date, customer_id, order_total, and status. The customers table includes customer details, such as customer_id, first_name, last_name, email, and city.

We will use the following SQL techniques to answer different business questions.

1. Retrieve Orders with Total Greater Than $100

To find all orders where the order total is greater than $100:

sql

```
SELECT * FROM orders
WHERE order_total > 100;
```

2. Retrieve Orders Placed in 2023 for a Specific Customer

To find all orders placed by a customer (with customer_id 1) in 2023:

sql

```
SELECT * FROM orders
WHERE customer_id = 1
AND order_date BETWEEN '2023-01-01' AND '2023-12-31';
```

3. Retrieve Orders from 'New York' and 'Los Angeles'

To find all orders placed by customers from **New York** or **Los Angeles**:

sql

```
SELECT * FROM orders
WHERE customer_id IN (SELECT customer_id FROM
customers WHERE city IN ('New York', 'Los
Angeles'));
```

4. Retrieve Orders with Pending Status

To retrieve orders that are **pending**:

sql

```
SELECT * FROM orders
WHERE status = 'Pending';
```

5. Retrieve Products with 'Laptop' in the Name

To retrieve products with the word "Laptop" in their name:

sql

```
SELECT * FROM products
WHERE product_name LIKE '%Laptop%';
```

Conclusion

In this chapter, we've learned how to filter data in SQL using various techniques:

- **Comparison operators** for simple conditions.

- **Logical operators** (AND, OR, NOT) to combine multiple conditions.
- Advanced filtering techniques like **IN, BETWEEN, LIKE**, and **IS NULL** to handle more complex queries.
- **Real-world examples** of querying orders in a sales system demonstrate how these techniques can be applied to practical scenarios.

These foundational skills will serve as the backbone for more advanced SQL queries and optimizations that we will explore in future chapters. In the next chapter, we'll dive deeper into **aggregating data** using functions like COUNT, SUM, AVG, and GROUP BY, to summarize and analyze large datasets efficiently.

CHAPTER 6

AGGREGATING DATA: GROUP BY AND HAVING

As your SQL queries become more complex, you'll often need to **aggregate** data to summarize and analyze it. **Aggregation** refers to calculating a single value that represents a group of values. SQL provides several functions for this purpose, such as COUNT(), SUM(), AVG(), MAX(), and MIN().

In this chapter, we will focus on the key concepts of **grouping data** with GROUP BY and filtering grouped data using the HAVING clause. You will learn how to apply these concepts to perform **real-world analysis**, such as generating sales reports for products.

1. Counting, Summing, Averaging, and Finding Maximum/Minimum

SQL provides several **aggregate functions** that perform operations on groups of data. Let's look at these functions in more detail:

1.1. COUNT()

The COUNT () function returns the number of rows that match a specified condition. It is often used to count the number of records in a table or group of records.

```sql
SELECT COUNT(*) FROM orders;
```

This query will return the total number of orders in the orders table.

If you want to count the number of orders per customer, you would use COUNT () with GROUP BY (explained below).

1.2. SUM()

The SUM () function returns the total sum of a numeric column. It is useful for calculating total sales, total revenue, or any other sum of a numeric field.

```sql
SELECT SUM(order_total) FROM orders;
```

This query will return the total value of all orders in the orders table.

1.3. AVG()

The AVG() function calculates the average value of a numeric column. This is helpful for finding the average price of products, average order value, etc.

sql

```
SELECT AVG(order_total) FROM orders;
```

This query will return the average value of all orders in the orders table.

1.4. MAX() and MIN()

The MAX() function returns the maximum value from a numeric column, while the MIN() function returns the minimum value.

sql

```
SELECT MAX(order_total) FROM orders;
```

This query will return the highest order total in the orders table.

sql

```
SELECT MIN(order_total) FROM orders;
```

This query will return the lowest order total in the orders table.

2. Grouping Data with GROUP BY

The GROUP BY clause is used to group rows that have the same values in one or more columns. Once data is grouped, you can apply aggregate functions like COUNT(), SUM(), AVG(), MAX(), and MIN() to summarize the data.

Basic GROUP BY Syntax:

sql

```
SELECT column1, aggregate_function(column2)
FROM table_name
GROUP BY column1;
```

- column1: The column by which the data is grouped.
- aggregate_function(column2): The aggregate function you want to apply to another column (e.g., COUNT(), SUM(), AVG()).

Example: Counting the Number of Orders by Customer

To count the number of orders each customer has placed, you would use the COUNT() function and GROUP BY the customer_id column:

sql

```
SELECT customer_id, COUNT(*) AS num_orders
FROM orders
GROUP BY customer_id;
```

This query returns the number of orders placed by each customer. The result might look like this:

customer_id	num_orders
1	5
2	3
3	8

Example: Summing the Total Sales by Product

To calculate the total sales for each product (i.e., sum of order_total for each product), we would use:

sql

```
SELECT    product_id,    SUM(order_total)    AS
total_sales
FROM orders
GROUP BY product_id;
```

This query returns the total sales for each product.

3. Filtering Grouped Data with HAVING

The HAVING clause is similar to the WHERE clause, but it is used to filter records **after** the aggregation has been performed. While WHERE filters rows before aggregation, HAVING filters the results of an aggregation.

Basic HAVING Syntax:
sql

```
SELECT column1, aggregate_function(column2)
FROM table_name
GROUP BY column1
HAVING aggregate_function(column2) condition;
```

- condition: The condition used to filter the grouped results (e.g., SUM(order_total) > 1000).

Example: Filtering Products with Total Sales Greater Than $1000

If you want to find products that have generated total sales greater than $1000, you can use the HAVING clause to filter the grouped results:

sql

```
SELECT     product_id,     SUM(order_total)     AS
total_sales
FROM orders
```

```
GROUP BY product_id
HAVING SUM(order_total) > 1000;
```

This query will return products whose total sales exceed $1000.

Example: Finding Customers with More Than 3 Orders

To find customers who have placed more than 3 orders, you can combine COUNT() with HAVING:

sql

```
SELECT customer_id, COUNT(*) AS num_orders
FROM orders
GROUP BY customer_id
HAVING COUNT(*) > 3;
```

This query will return customers who have placed more than 3 orders.

---

4. Real-World Example: Generating Sales Reports for Products

Let's apply the concepts from this chapter to a real-world scenario: generating sales reports for products in an e-commerce system. Suppose we have two tables: **orders** and **order_items**.

- **orders**: Contains general order information (e.g., `order_id`, `order_date`, `customer_id`).
- **order_items**: Contains details of each item ordered, such as `order_id`, `product_id`, `quantity`, and `price`.

We want to generate a sales report that includes:

- Total sales per product.
- The number of orders for each product.
- The average order value for each product.

Step 1: Total Sales by Product

To find the total sales for each product, we need to join the `orders` and `order_items` tables, then group by `product_id` and sum the order totals.

sql

```
SELECT    oi.product_id,    SUM(oi.quantity    *
oi.price) AS total_sales
FROM order_items oi
JOIN orders o ON oi.order_id = o.order_id
GROUP BY oi.product_id
ORDER BY total_sales DESC;
```

This query calculates the total sales for each product by multiplying the quantity and price of each item ordered. It groups the data by `product_id` and sorts the result in descending order of total sales.

Step 2: Number of Orders per Product

Next, let's calculate the number of orders for each product. We can use the COUNT() function:

sql

```
SELECT oi.product_id, COUNT(DISTINCT o.order_id)
AS num_orders
FROM order_items oi
JOIN orders o ON oi.order_id = o.order_id
GROUP BY oi.product_id;
```

This query counts the distinct number of orders (`order_id`) for each `product_id`.

Step 3: Average Order Value per Product

To find the average order value for each product, we calculate the average of the order totals:

sql

```
SELECT    oi.product_id,    AVG(oi.quantity    *
oi.price) AS avg_order_value
FROM order_items oi
```

```
JOIN orders o ON oi.order_id = o.order_id
GROUP BY oi.product_id;
```

This query calculates the average order value for each product by averaging the total price (`quantity * price`) per product.

Step 4: Putting It All Together

Finally, we can combine all of these calculations into a single query to generate a comprehensive sales report:

sql

```
SELECT oi.product_id,
       SUM(oi.quantity    *    oi.price)    AS
total_sales,
       COUNT(DISTINCT o.order_id) AS num_orders,
       AVG(oi.quantity    *    oi.price)    AS
avg_order_value
FROM order_items oi
JOIN orders o ON oi.order_id = o.order_id
GROUP BY oi.product_id
HAVING total_sales > 1000
ORDER BY total_sales DESC;
```

This query will return a sales report that shows:

- The `total_sales` for each product.
- The `num_orders` for each product.

- The `avg_order_value` for each product.
- Only products with total sales greater than $1000 are included, and the results are ordered by `total_sales` in descending order.

Conclusion

In this chapter, we explored how to **aggregate data** using SQL's powerful aggregate functions (`COUNT()`, `SUM()`, `AVG()`, `MAX()`, and `MIN()`). We learned how to **group data** with the `GROUP BY` clause and **filter grouped data** with the `HAVING` clause. These techniques allow you to perform advanced data analysis, such as generating detailed sales reports and summarizing large datasets.

Through the **real-world example** of generating sales reports, we demonstrated how to apply these techniques to build insightful and actionable reports. In the next chapter, we will dive deeper into **joining tables** and combining data from multiple sources, which is essential for building more complex queries in relational databases.

CHAPTER 7

JOINING TABLES: COMBINING DATA FROM MULTIPLE SOURCES

As you work with relational databases, you will often need to combine data from multiple tables. This is where **joins** come into play. SQL joins allow you to retrieve and combine data from two or more tables based on related columns. In this chapter, we will explore various types of **joins**, including **INNER JOIN, LEFT JOIN, RIGHT JOIN**, and **FULL OUTER JOIN**, as well as **self-joins** and **cross joins**. Additionally, we'll learn how to use **table aliases** to make complex queries easier to read and write.

By the end of this chapter, you'll have the tools to combine data from multiple tables and create powerful queries that reflect complex relationships between your data.

1. INNER JOIN: Combining Matching Rows

The **INNER JOIN** is the most common type of join in SQL. It returns only the rows that have matching values in both tables. If there is no match, those rows are excluded from the result.

Basic INNER JOIN Syntax:

sql

```
SELECT column1, column2
FROM table1
INNER JOIN table2 ON table1.column_name =
table2.column_name;
```

- `INNER JOIN`: Specifies the type of join.
- `table1.column_name = table2.column_name`: The condition that matches rows from both tables.

Example: Retrieving User and Order Data

Let's say we have two tables in a marketplace application: **users** and **orders**. We want to retrieve information about users and their corresponding orders.

users table:

84

user_id	first_name	last_name
1	Alice	Johnson
2	Bob	Smith
3	Charlie	Brown

orders table:

order_id	user_id	product_name	order_date
101	1	Laptop	2023-10-01
102	2	Smartphone	2023-10-02
103	1	Tablet	2023-10-03

To get a list of all users who have placed an order, along with the product name and order date, you would use an **INNER JOIN**:

sql

```
SELECT    users.first_name,    users.last_name,
orders.product_name, orders.order_date
FROM users
INNER    JOIN    orders    ON    users.user_id    =
orders.user_id;
```

Example Output:

first_name last_name product_name order_date

Alice	Johnson	Laptop	2023-10-01
Bob	Smith	Smartphone	2023-10-02
Alice	Johnson	Tablet	2023-10-03

---

2. LEFT JOIN: Including All Rows from the Left Table

The **LEFT JOIN** (also called **LEFT OUTER JOIN**) returns all the rows from the left table, even if there is no match in the right table. If there is no match, NULL values will be returned for the columns from the right table.

Basic LEFT JOIN Syntax:
sql

```
SELECT column1, column2
FROM table1
LEFT JOIN table2 ON table1.column_name = table2.column_name;
```

Example: Retrieving All Users and Their Orders

If you want to list all users, including those who haven't placed any orders, you would use a **LEFT JOIN**:

sql

```
SELECT    users.first_name,    users.last_name,
orders.product_name, orders.order_date
FROM users
LEFT    JOIN    orders    ON    users.user_id    =
orders.user_id;
```

Example Output:

first_name	last_name	product_name	order_date
Alice	Johnson	Laptop	2023-10-01
Alice	Johnson	Tablet	2023-10-03
Bob	Smith	Smartphone	2023-10-02
Charlie	Brown	NULL	NULL

Notice that Charlie is included in the result, even though they have no orders. For this user, the columns from the **orders** table are NULL.

---

3. RIGHT JOIN: Including All Rows from the Right Table

The **RIGHT JOIN** (also called **RIGHT OUTER JOIN**) returns all rows from the right table, and the matching rows from the left table. If there's no match, NULL values will be returned for columns from the left table.

Basic RIGHT JOIN Syntax:
sql

```
SELECT column1, column2
FROM table1
RIGHT JOIN table2 ON table1.column_name =
table2.column_name;
```

Example: Retrieving All Orders and Their Corresponding Users

If you wanted to list all orders, including those without any corresponding user data (for example, orders that may be missing a user_id), you would use a **RIGHT JOIN**:

sql

```
SELECT    users.first_name,    users.last_name,
orders.product_name, orders.order_date
FROM users
RIGHT JOIN orders ON users.user_id =
orders.user_id;
```

Example Output:

first_name last_name product_name order_date

Alice   Johnson   Laptop   2023-10-01

first_name	last_name	product_name	order_date
Bob	Smith	Smartphone	2023-10-02
Alice	Johnson	Tablet	2023-10-03

4. FULL OUTER JOIN: Combining All Rows from Both Tables

The **FULL OUTER JOIN** returns all rows when there is a match in one of the tables. It returns NULL for non-matching rows from both tables. It's useful when you want to see all data, whether or not a match exists.

Basic FULL OUTER JOIN Syntax:
sql

```
SELECT column1, column2
FROM table1
FULL OUTER JOIN table2 ON table1.column_name =
table2.column_name;
```

Example: Combining All Users and Orders

To get a full list of both users and orders, including those users who have not placed orders and orders that do not have associated users, you would use a **FULL OUTER JOIN**:

sql

```
SELECT     users.first_name,     users.last_name,
orders.product_name, orders.order_date
FROM users
FULL   OUTER   JOIN   orders   ON   users.user_id   =
orders.user_id;
```

Example Output:

first_name	last_name	product_name	order_date
Alice	Johnson	Laptop	2023-10-01
Alice	Johnson	Tablet	2023-10-03
Bob	Smith	Smartphone	2023-10-02
Charlie	Brown	NULL	NULL

Here, you would see all users, all orders, and any missing values for users or orders.

---

5. Self-Joins: Joining a Table to Itself

A **self-join** is a join where a table is joined to itself. This is typically useful when you need to compare rows within the same table.

Example: Finding Employee Managers

Let's say we have an **employees** table where each employee has a `manager_id` that refers to the `employee_id` of their manager. To find each employee and their manager's name, we can perform a self-join:

sql

```
SELECT   e.employee_name,   m.employee_name   AS
manager_name
FROM employees e
LEFT   JOIN   employees   m   ON   e.manager_id   =
m.employee_id;
```

Here, the **employees** table is being joined to itself. The alias e refers to the employee, and the alias m refers to the manager.

---

6. Cross Joins: Creating a Cartesian Product

A **CROSS JOIN** returns the Cartesian product of two tables. This means that it combines every row from the first table with every row from the second table, regardless of matching values.

Basic CROSS JOIN Syntax:

sql

```
SELECT column1, column2
```

```
FROM table1
CROSS JOIN table2;
```

Example: Generating All Possible Combinations of Products and Customers

Suppose you want to generate all possible combinations of products and customers. A CROSS JOIN can be used:

sql

```
SELECT                    products.product_name,
customers.first_name
FROM products
CROSS JOIN customers;
```

This will give you all possible combinations of products and customers. Be careful, as this can result in a very large result set if both tables are large.

---

7. Using Aliases for Tables and Columns

Using **aliases** for tables and columns is crucial when working with complex queries. Aliases make your queries easier to read and help avoid ambiguity, especially when joining multiple tables.

Basic Alias Syntax:

sql

```
SELECT t1.column1, t2.column2
FROM table1 AS t1
JOIN   table2   AS   t2   ON   t1.column_name   =
t2.column_name;
```

- `AS t1` and `AS t2`: Aliases for `table1` and `table2` to make the query more concise.

Example: Using Aliases in Joins

Here's how to use aliases in a query to join **users** and **orders**:

sql

```
SELECT          u.first_name,          u.last_name,
o.product_name, o.order_date
FROM users AS u
INNER JOIN orders AS o ON u.user_id = o.user_id;
```

In this example, `u` is an alias for `users`, and `o` is an alias for `orders`.

Real-World Example: Combining User and Order Data in a Marketplace Application

Now, let's combine everything we've learned to create a real-world example. We have two tables: **users** and **orders**. Our goal is to generate a report that includes each user's name and the products they've ordered.

Tables:

users:

user_id	first_name	last_name
1	Alice	Johnson
2	Bob	Smith

orders:

order_id	user_id	product_name	order_date
101	1	Laptop	2023-10-01
102	2	Smartphone	2023-10-02

Query: Combine User and Order Data

sql

```sql
SELECT        u.first_name,        u.last_name,
o.product_name, o.order_date
FROM users AS u
```

```
INNER JOIN orders AS o ON u.user_id = o.user_id;
```

Result:

first_name	last_name	product_name	order_date
Alice	Johnson	Laptop	2023-10-01
Bob	Smith	Smartphone	2023-10-02

This query combines data from the **users** and **orders** tables using an `INNER JOIN` based on the `user_id` field, providing a complete list of products ordered by users.

Conclusion

In this chapter, we explored how to combine data from multiple tables using different types of joins. We covered:

- **INNER JOIN** for retrieving matching rows.
- **LEFT JOIN** and **RIGHT JOIN** for including all rows from one table, even when there's no match.
- **FULL OUTER JOIN** for including all rows from both tables.
- **Self-joins** for joining a table to itself.
- **CROSS JOIN** for generating a Cartesian product.
- **Using aliases** to make complex queries more readable.

By applying these techniques to real-world scenarios, such as combining user and order data in a marketplace application, you can build powerful, data-driven queries to generate reports and insights.

In the next chapter, we will explore more advanced techniques for manipulating and aggregating data, including **subqueries** and **nested queries**.

CHAPTER 8

SUBQUERIES: WRITING QUERIES INSIDE QUERIES

In SQL, you often encounter situations where you need to retrieve data based on the result of another query. This is where **subqueries** come into play. A **subquery** is a query nested inside another query. It allows you to use the result of one query to filter, join, or manipulate data in the outer query. Subqueries are a powerful tool for tackling complex queries that would be cumbersome to write with just joins or basic conditions.

In this chapter, we will explore the concept of subqueries, how they are used in various SQL clauses (like SELECT, FROM, and WHERE), the difference between **correlated** and **non-correlated subqueries**, and how to use them for advanced filtering. We'll also provide a **real-world example** of querying products sold by specific users to illustrate the power of subqueries.

1. Subqueries in SELECT, FROM, and WHERE Clauses

A subquery is simply a query that is nested inside another query. It can be used in several places, such as the SELECT, FROM, or WHERE clauses.

1.1. Subqueries in the SELECT Clause

A **subquery in the SELECT clause** allows you to calculate values based on another query for each row in the result set.

Example: Retrieving Product Prices with Average Price

Let's say we have a products table and we want to get the price of each product along with the average price of all products in the system:

sql

```
SELECT product_name, price,
      (SELECT AVG(price) FROM products) AS
avg_price
FROM products;
```

In this query:

- The subquery (SELECT AVG(price) FROM products) calculates the average price of all products.

98

- The result of the subquery is included in the output for each product.

1.2. Subqueries in the FROM Clause

A **subquery in the FROM clause** can be used to create a derived table (a temporary table) that can be used like any other table in the query. This is useful when you need to perform calculations or transformations before using the results in your main query.

Example: Subquery in FROM Clause for Total Sales per Product

Let's say we want to calculate the total sales for each product and then join it with the `products` table to get product details:

sql

```
SELECT p.product_name, t.total_sales
FROM products p
JOIN (SELECT product_id, SUM(order_total) AS
total_sales
     FROM orders
     GROUP BY product_id) t
ON p.product_id = t.product_id;
```

In this query:

- The subquery in the FROM clause calculates the total sales per product.
- This subquery is aliased as t and then joined with the products table on the product_id.

1.3. Subqueries in the WHERE Clause

The **WHERE clause** is the most common place to use subqueries. You can use a subquery in the WHERE clause to filter rows based on the result of another query.

Example: Find Customers Who Made Orders Over $500

If we want to find customers who have placed orders greater than $500, we can use a subquery in the WHERE clause:

sql

```sql
SELECT first_name, last_name
FROM customers
WHERE customer_id IN (SELECT customer_id
                      FROM orders
                      WHERE order_total > 500);
```

In this query:

- The subquery returns the customer_id for all orders greater than $500.

100

- The outer query retrieves the first and last names of customers whose `customer_id` appears in the subquery result.

---

2. Correlated vs. Non-Correlated Subqueries

Subqueries can be classified into two categories: **correlated** and **non-correlated** subqueries. Understanding the difference between these two is important for optimizing and correctly structuring your queries.

2.1. Non-Correlated Subqueries

A **non-correlated subquery** is a subquery that can be executed independently of the outer query. It does not rely on the outer query for its execution.

Example: Non-Correlated Subquery

sql

```
SELECT product_name, price
FROM products
WHERE price > (SELECT AVG(price) FROM products);
```

In this query:

- The subquery (`SELECT AVG(price) FROM products`) calculates the average price of all products.
- The result of this subquery is used in the `WHERE` clause to filter products that have a price higher than the average.

This is a **non-correlated subquery** because the subquery can be executed independently of the outer query.

2.2. Correlated Subqueries

A **correlated subquery** is a subquery that depends on the outer query. The subquery references columns from the outer query, and as a result, it cannot be executed independently.

Example: Correlated Subquery

sql

```
SELECT p.product_name, p.price
FROM products p
WHERE p.price > (SELECT AVG(price) FROM orders o
WHERE o.product_id = p.product_id);
```

In this query:

- The subquery references `p.product_id` from the outer query.
- The subquery calculates the average price for each product, and for each row in the `products` table, the

outer query compares the product's price to the average price of the corresponding product in the `orders` table.

Because the subquery depends on the value of `p.product_id` from the outer query, this is a **correlated subquery**.

---

3. Using Subqueries for Advanced Filtering

Subqueries can be used for advanced filtering operations, such as finding values that exist in one set but not in another, or applying multiple conditions that would be difficult to express with basic joins.

Example: Find Products Not Sold in Any Order

Let's say we want to find all products that have not been sold in any order. We can use a subquery to filter out products that have appeared in the `orders` table.

sql

```
SELECT product_name
FROM products
WHERE product_id NOT IN (SELECT DISTINCT
product_id FROM order_items);
```

In this query:

- The subquery retrieves all `product_ids` that have been sold at least once by querying the `order_items` table.
- The outer query selects products whose `product_id` is **not** in the list of sold products.

4. Real-World Example: Querying Products Sold by Specific Users

Now, let's take a look at a **real-world example**: Suppose we have a **marketplace application** with the following tables:

- **users**: Contains user information (e.g., `user_id`, `first_name`, `last_name`).
- **orders**: Contains order details (e.g., `order_id`, `user_id`, `order_date`).
- **order_items**: Contains the items ordered (e.g., `order_id`, `product_id`, `quantity`).
- **products**: Contains product details (e.g., `product_id`, `product_name`, `price`).

Our goal is to find all the products sold by **specific users**, say users with a `user_id` of 1 and 2.

Step 1: Querying Products Sold by Specific Users

To retrieve products sold by users with `user_id` 1 and 2, we can use a subquery in the WHERE clause:

sql

```
SELECT p.product_name
FROM products p
WHERE p.product_id IN (
    SELECT oi.product_id
    FROM order_items oi
    JOIN orders o ON oi.order_id = o.order_id
    WHERE o.user_id IN (1, 2)
);
```

Explanation:

- The **inner subquery** retrieves the `product_ids` from the `order_items` table for users with `user_id` 1 or 2.
- The **outer query** retrieves the `product_name` for those `product_ids` from the `products` table.

Example Output:

product_name

Laptop

Smartphone

product_name

Tablet

This query returns a list of products sold to users 1 and 2, as specified.

Conclusion

In this chapter, we covered how to use **subqueries** in SQL, which are queries nested inside other queries. Subqueries are powerful tools that allow you to perform operations that would be difficult with simple joins or filters. We explored:

- **Subqueries in the SELECT, FROM, and WHERE clauses** for different use cases.
- The difference between **correlated** and **non-correlated subqueries**.
- How to use subqueries for **advanced filtering** operations.
- A **real-world example** of querying products sold by specific users in a marketplace application.

Subqueries help you solve complex problems by allowing you to nest queries and filter data based on results from other queries. In the next chapter, we will dive deeper into **advanced SQL**

techniques, such as **window functions** and **common table expressions (CTEs)**, to further enhance your query-writing skills.

CHAPTER 9

UNION AND UNION ALL: COMBINING RESULTS FROM MULTIPLE QUERIES

SQL provides powerful ways to combine the results of multiple queries into a single result set. One of the most common methods for doing this is through the **UNION** and **UNION ALL** operators. These operators allow you to merge the results of two or more SELECT queries. This chapter will explain how **UNION** and **UNION ALL** work, the differences between them, and how to use them to combine data from different tables or sources. We will also explore a **real-world example** of merging data from different regions in a global business database.

---

1. UNION and UNION ALL: Combining Results from Multiple Queries

Both UNION and UNION ALL are used to combine the results of two or more queries into one result set. However, they differ in how they handle duplicate records.

1.1. UNION

The UNION operator combines the result sets of two or more SELECT queries and **removes duplicate rows** from the final result. In other words, it returns only distinct rows across all queries.

Syntax:
sql

```
SELECT column1, column2, ...
FROM table1
UNION
SELECT column1, column2, ...
FROM table2;
```

- UNION combines the results of both SELECT queries and eliminates any duplicate rows.
- Both SELECT queries must have the same number of columns, and the corresponding columns must have compatible data types.

Example: Combining Customer Names from Two Different Tables

Let's say you have two tables: us_customers and eu_customers, both with the same structure, storing customer names from different regions. To retrieve a combined list of distinct customer names from both regions, you would use UNION:

```
sql
```

```
SELECT first_name, last_name
FROM us_customers
UNION
SELECT first_name, last_name
FROM eu_customers;
```

This query combines the results of both tables and removes any duplicate customer names.

1.2. UNION ALL

The UNION ALL operator, unlike UNION, combines the results of two or more SELECT queries but **includes all rows**, including duplicates. It is generally faster than UNION because it does not need to perform the additional work of removing duplicate rows.

Syntax:
```
sql
```

```
SELECT column1, column2, ...
FROM table1
UNION ALL
SELECT column1, column2, ...
FROM table2;
```

- UNION ALL combines the result sets of the queries and includes all records, even if they are duplicates.

- As with UNION, both queries must have the same number of columns and compatible data types.

Example: Combining All Customer Names from Both Regions (Including Duplicates)

If you want to retrieve all customer names from both the us_customers and eu_customers tables, including duplicates (for example, customers who are listed in both regions), you would use UNION ALL:

sql

```
SELECT first_name, last_name
FROM us_customers
UNION ALL
SELECT first_name, last_name
FROM eu_customers;
```

This query will include duplicate customer names if they exist in both tables.

---

2. Difference between UNION and UNION ALL

The primary difference between UNION and UNION ALL is how they handle duplicate records:

Feature	UNION	UNION ALL
Duplicates	Removes duplicate rows	Includes all rows, even duplicates
Performance	Slower (due to deduplication)	Faster (no deduplication)
Use Case	When you need unique records only	When you want all records, including duplicates

- **UNION** is useful when you need a distinct set of results and want to eliminate duplicate rows across queries.
- **UNION ALL** is preferred when duplicates are acceptable or desired, and you want to include every row from each query, making it more efficient.

---

3. Combining Data from Different Tables

You can use UNION and UNION ALL to combine data from different tables, provided that the tables have the same number of columns and matching data types. This is especially useful when working with partitioned data or combining similar datasets from different sources.

Example: Combining Data from Multiple Tables

Suppose you have three tables, `sales_q1`, `sales_q2`, and `sales_q3`, and each table contains sales data for different quarters. To retrieve all sales data from the three quarters, you can use `UNION ALL` to include all rows:

sql

```
SELECT product_id, total_sales, quarter
FROM sales_q1
UNION ALL
SELECT product_id, total_sales, quarter
FROM sales_q2
UNION ALL
SELECT product_id, total_sales, quarter
FROM sales_q3;
```

This query will return sales data from all three quarters, including duplicates, since `UNION ALL` is used.

---

4. Real-World Example: Merging Data from Different Regions in a Global Business Database

Let's consider a **global business database** that stores sales data from different regions. The business operates in multiple countries, and each country maintains its own sales table. We want

113

to combine sales data from these different regions into one unified report.

Example Tables:

- **us_sales**: Contains sales data for the United States.
- **eu_sales**: Contains sales data for Europe.
- **asia_sales**: Contains sales data for Asia.

Each table contains columns like `region`, `product_id`, `sales_amount`, and `sales_date`.

Step 1: Combining Sales Data from Different Regions

We want to generate a report of all sales across the three regions, including all data. We can use UNION ALL to include all records:

sql

```
SELECT     region,     product_id,     sales_amount,
sales_date
FROM us_sales
UNION ALL
SELECT     region,     product_id,     sales_amount,
sales_date
FROM eu_sales
UNION ALL
SELECT     region,     product_id,     sales_amount,
sales_date
```

```
FROM asia_sales;
```

This query combines sales data from all three regions and includes all rows, including duplicates. The result will contain all sales records from the United States, Europe, and Asia.

Step 2: Filtering Data for a Specific Region or Date Range

If we want to filter the combined data to show only sales from the us_sales table, we can add a WHERE clause:

sql

```
SELECT    region,    product_id,    sales_amount,
sales_date
FROM us_sales
UNION ALL
SELECT    region,    product_id,    sales_amount,
sales_date
FROM eu_sales
UNION ALL
SELECT    region,    product_id,    sales_amount,
sales_date
FROM asia_sales
WHERE sales_date BETWEEN '2023-01-01' AND '2023-
12-31';
```

This query filters the sales data for the year 2023, from all three regions.

Step 3: Removing Duplicates with UNION

If we want to ensure that we only get unique sales records across all regions (i.e., remove any duplicates), we can replace UNION ALL with UNION:

```sql
SELECT    region,    product_id,    sales_amount,
sales_date
FROM us_sales
UNION
SELECT    region,    product_id,    sales_amount,
sales_date
FROM eu_sales
UNION
SELECT    region,    product_id,    sales_amount,
sales_date
FROM asia_sales;
```

This query will return only distinct sales records across all regions.

Conclusion

In this chapter, we've learned how to use the **UNION** and **UNION ALL** operators to combine the results of multiple queries. Here are the key takeaways:

- **UNION** combines results and removes duplicates, while **UNION ALL** includes all rows, even duplicates.

- Both operators can be used to combine data from different **tables**, as long as the tables have the same number of columns and compatible data types.

- **Real-world example**: We explored how to combine sales data from different regions in a global business database and filter or aggregate this data for reporting purposes.

By mastering the use of UNION and UNION ALL, you'll be able to merge data from multiple sources and generate comprehensive reports that aggregate data across your database. In the next chapter, we'll explore **window functions** and **common table expressions (CTEs)**, which offer even more powerful ways to analyze data across partitions and subqueries.

CHAPTER 10

MODIFYING DATA: INSERT, UPDATE, DELETE

In SQL, the ability to modify data is a fundamental task that every developer needs to master. SQL provides a set of commands that allow you to **insert, update**, and **delete** data within a database. These commands are essential for managing and maintaining dynamic datasets.

In this chapter, we will cover the following SQL commands:

- **INSERT**: Adding new data to a table.
- **UPDATE**: Modifying existing data in a table.
- **DELETE**: Removing data from a table.

We'll also work through a **real-world example** of managing customer records in a loyalty program, which will demonstrate how to use these SQL commands in a practical scenario.

1. Inserting Data into Tables

The **INSERT** statement is used to add new rows of data into a table. When you use INSERT, you specify the table into which you want to insert data and the values to be inserted.

Basic INSERT Syntax:
sql

```
INSERT   INTO   table_name   (column1,   column2,
column3, ...)
VALUES (value1, value2, value3, ...);
```

- table_name: The name of the table where data will be inserted.
- column1, column2, column3, ...: The columns where you want to insert values.
- value1, value2, value3, ...: The corresponding values for the columns.

Example: Inserting a New Customer into a Loyalty Program

Suppose we have a customers table in our loyalty program database, with columns customer_id, first_name, last_name, and email. To insert a new customer into the table:

sql

119

```
INSERT INTO customers (first_name, last_name,
email)
VALUES            ('Alice',            'Johnson',
'alice.johnson@example.com');
```

This query will add a new row to the `customers` table with the provided customer details.

Inserting Multiple Rows

You can insert multiple rows in a single `INSERT` statement by separating each set of values with commas:

sql

```
INSERT INTO customers (first_name, last_name,
email)
VALUES
  ('Bob', 'Smith', 'bob.smith@example.com'),
  ('Charlie',                          'Brown',
'charlie.brown@example.com'),
  ('David', 'Davis', 'david.davis@example.com');
```

This query inserts three new customers into the `customers` table at once.

2. Updating Existing Data

The **UPDATE** statement is used to modify the existing records in a table. When you use UPDATE, you must specify which rows to modify and what new values to assign.

Basic UPDATE Syntax:

```sql

UPDATE table_name
SET column1 = value1, column2 = value2, ...
WHERE condition;
```

- table_name: The name of the table where you want to modify data.
- column1, column2, ...: The columns whose values you want to update.
- value1, value2, ...: The new values to assign to the columns.
- WHERE condition: A condition to identify the rows that should be updated. **Without a WHERE clause, all rows in the table will be updated**, so it's essential to use it carefully.

Example: Updating a Customer's Email in the Loyalty Program

Let's say we want to update the email address for a specific customer (with customer_id = 1):

121

sql

```
UPDATE customers
SET email = 'alice.johnson@newdomain.com'
WHERE customer_id = 1;
```

This query updates the email address for the customer with customer_id 1 to alice.johnson@newdomain.com.

Updating Multiple Columns

You can update multiple columns at once by separating each column and value with a comma:

sql

```
UPDATE customers
SET first_name = 'Alice', last_name = 'Green',
email = 'alice.green@example.com'
WHERE customer_id = 1;
```

This query updates the first_name, last_name, and email for the customer with customer_id 1.

---

3. Deleting Data from Tables

The **DELETE** statement is used to remove one or more rows from a table. It's important to note that **DELETE** permanently removes the data, and this operation cannot be undone unless you have backups.

Basic DELETE Syntax:

sql

```
DELETE FROM table_name
WHERE condition;
```

- table_name: The name of the table from which to delete data.
- WHERE condition: A condition to specify which rows to delete. **Without a WHERE clause, all rows in the table will be deleted**, so be cautious when using this command.

Example: Deleting a Customer from the Loyalty Program

Let's say we want to delete the customer with customer_id 1 from the customers table:

sql

```
DELETE FROM customers
WHERE customer_id = 1;
```

This query will delete the row where customer_id is 1. The customer record will be permanently removed.

Deleting All Records

If you want to delete all rows in a table (but keep the table structure intact), you can omit the WHERE clause:

```sql

DELETE FROM customers;
```

This query will remove all customer records from the customers table.

---

4. Real-World Example: Managing Customer Records in a Loyalty Program

Let's imagine we have a **loyalty program** for a retail company, and we're managing customer records in the database. We have a customers table that stores customer information such as their names, email addresses, and loyalty points.

Here's a summary of what we want to do in our loyalty program:

1. **Insert** new customers who have joined the program.
2. **Update** the details of existing customers, like email addresses or loyalty points.

3. **Delete** customers who request to be removed from the loyalty program.

Step 1: Inserting New Customers

As customers join the loyalty program, we insert their data into the customers table:

sql

```
INSERT INTO customers (first_name, last_name,
email, loyalty_points)
VALUES           ('Emma',           'Wilson',
'emma.wilson@example.com', 150);
```

This query adds a new customer named Emma Wilson with 150 loyalty points.

Step 2: Updating Existing Customer Information

If Emma updates her email address, we can modify the existing record:

sql

```
UPDATE customers
SET email = 'emma.wilson@newdomain.com'
WHERE first_name = 'Emma' AND last_name =
'Wilson';
```

125

This query updates Emma Wilson's email address in the database.

Step 3: Deleting Customer Data

If a customer requests to be removed from the loyalty program, we can delete their record:

sql

```
DELETE FROM customers
WHERE customer_id = 2;
```

This query removes the customer with `customer_id` 2 from the loyalty program.

Step 4: Managing Loyalty Points (Update Example)

If Emma earns additional loyalty points, we can update her `loyalty_points`:

sql

```
UPDATE customers
SET loyalty_points = loyalty_points + 50
WHERE first_name = 'Emma' AND last_name =
'Wilson';
```

This query adds 50 points to Emma's existing balance.

Conclusion

In this chapter, we covered the essential **data-modifying operations** in SQL:

- **INSERT**: Adding new rows to a table.
- **UPDATE**: Modifying existing rows in a table.
- **DELETE**: Removing rows from a table.

We also explored a **real-world example** of managing customer records in a loyalty program. Understanding how to use INSERT, UPDATE, and DELETE commands is fundamental for maintaining and manipulating data in any SQL-based system.

In the next chapter, we will dive into **advanced SQL topics** such as **joins**, **subqueries**, and **aggregating data** to further enhance your SQL querying skills and enable you to work with more complex datasets.

CHAPTER 11

TRANSACTIONS IN SQL: ENSURING DATA INTEGRITY

SQL transactions are critical for ensuring that data operations in a database are completed successfully and in a consistent state. **Transactions** allow multiple database operations to be executed as a single unit of work, ensuring that they are **atomic, consistent, isolated**, and **durable** — collectively known as the **ACID properties**.

In this chapter, we will explore the concept of **transactions**, how they ensure **data integrity**, and how to manage them using SQL commands like COMMIT and ROLLBACK. We will also discuss **transaction isolation levels**, which determine how transactions interact with each other.

We'll end with a **real-world example** of implementing **bank transfers** in a banking system to illustrate how transactions ensure consistency in a real-world application.

1. ACID Properties of Transactions

The term **ACID** refers to the four key properties that transactions must satisfy to ensure data integrity:

- **A**: **Atomicity** — A transaction is atomic, meaning it is treated as a single unit. Either all operations in the transaction are completed, or none are. If one part of the transaction fails, the entire transaction is rolled back.
- **C**: **Consistency** — A transaction brings the database from one valid state to another. The database must always remain in a consistent state before and after the transaction.
- **I**: **Isolation** — Each transaction is isolated from others, meaning that the intermediate state of a transaction is not visible to other transactions. Transactions may be executed concurrently but without affecting each other's results.
- **D**: **Durability** — Once a transaction is committed, its changes are permanent, even in the case of system failures. The changes are saved to disk.

Example of ACID Properties:

Consider a bank transfer operation where money is being moved from one account to another. If the system crashes after subtracting the amount from the sender's account but before adding it to the recipient's account, the transaction would be rolled back to maintain consistency and atomicity.

---

2. COMMIT and ROLLBACK Statements

In SQL, **transactions** begin automatically when you perform an action on the database, but you need to explicitly **commit** or **rollback** the transaction to finalize or undo the changes.

2.1. COMMIT Statement

The COMMIT statement is used to save the changes made by a transaction permanently to the database. Once a transaction is committed, the changes cannot be undone.

Syntax:
sql

```
COMMIT;
```

Example: Committing a Transaction

Let's say we are updating a customer's email address and then committing the changes:

sql

```
BEGIN;
```

```
UPDATE customers
SET email = 'new.email@example.com'
WHERE customer_id = 1;
```

```
COMMIT;
```

This transaction updates the customer's email address and then commits the changes, making them permanent.

2.2. ROLLBACK Statement

The ROLLBACK statement is used to undo all changes made by the transaction. This is useful when you encounter an error or if you decide to cancel the transaction.

Syntax:
```sql
```

```
ROLLBACK;
```

Example: Rolling Back a Transaction

If we encounter an error while updating a customer's email address, we can roll back the transaction to restore the previous state:

```sql
```

```
BEGIN;

UPDATE customers
SET email = 'new.email@example.com'
WHERE customer_id = 1;

-- Some error occurs

ROLLBACK;
```

In this example, the changes made to the `customers` table are undone, and the email remains unchanged.

---

3. Managing Transaction Isolation Levels

SQL provides different **isolation levels** that define how transactions interact with each other. Isolation levels determine the visibility of uncommitted data to other transactions and control issues such as **dirty reads, non-repeatable reads**, and **phantom reads**.

3.1. Isolation Levels

There are four standard isolation levels, each providing a different balance between **performance** and **data consistency**:

- **READ UNCOMMITTED**: The lowest isolation level, allowing transactions to read uncommitted changes made by other transactions. This can lead to **dirty reads**.

- **READ COMMITTED**: Ensures that transactions can only read committed data. However, this can still allow **non-repeatable reads** (data that can change between reads).

- **REPEATABLE READ**: Guarantees that if a transaction reads a piece of data, it will see the same value in subsequent reads during the transaction. However, **phantom reads** (new rows appearing) may still occur.

- **SERIALIZABLE**: The highest isolation level, ensuring complete isolation between transactions. This prevents **dirty reads**, **non-repeatable reads**, and **phantom reads** but can be less efficient.

3.2. Setting the Isolation Level

You can set the isolation level for a session in most relational database systems. For example, to set the isolation level to READ COMMITTED:

sql

```
SET TRANSACTION ISOLATION LEVEL READ COMMITTED;
```

This would ensure that the transaction only reads data that has been committed.

133

4. Real-World Example: Implementing Bank Transfers in a Banking System

Let's implement a **bank transfer** operation in a banking system. In this scenario, we have two tables:

- **accounts**: Contains `account_id`, `account_holder`, and `balance`.
- **transactions**: Contains `transaction_id`, `from_account`, `to_account`, `amount`, and `transaction_date`.

The goal is to transfer money from one account to another. This requires two operations:

1. Subtracting the amount from the sender's account.
2. Adding the amount to the recipient's account.

These operations must be part of a single transaction to ensure **atomicity** and **consistency**. If an error occurs during the transfer (e.g., insufficient funds or a system crash), we need to **rollback** the transaction.

Step 1: Begin the Transaction

We start by beginning a transaction:

sql

BEGIN;

Step 2: Check Sufficient Balance

Before transferring the funds, we check if the sender has sufficient balance:

sql

```
SELECT balance FROM accounts WHERE account_id =
1;
```

If the balance is sufficient, proceed to the next steps. If not, we **rollback** the transaction.

Step 3: Deduct Amount from Sender's Account

If the sender has sufficient funds, we subtract the amount from their account:

sql

```
UPDATE accounts
SET balance = balance - 100
WHERE account_id = 1;
```

Step 4: Add Amount to Recipient's Account

Next, we add the amount to the recipient's account:

```sql
sql
```

```sql
UPDATE accounts
SET balance = balance + 100
WHERE account_id = 2;
```

Step 5: Record the Transaction

We then insert a record of the transaction into the **transactions** table:

```sql
sql
```

```sql
INSERT     INTO     transactions     (from_account,
to_account, amount, transaction_date)
VALUES (1, 2, 100, NOW());
```

Step 6: Commit the Transaction

If all operations are successful, we **commit** the transaction to make the changes permanent:

```sql
sql
```

```sql
COMMIT;
```

Step 7: Rollback in Case of an Error

If any error occurs (e.g., insufficient funds or a database failure), we can **rollback** the transaction:

```sql
sql
```

```
ROLLBACK;
```

This will ensure that the entire transaction is undone and no partial changes are made to the database.

Conclusion

In this chapter, we discussed the importance of **transactions** in SQL and how they ensure **data integrity**. We covered the following concepts:

- **ACID properties**: Atomicity, Consistency, Isolation, and Durability.
- **COMMIT** and **ROLLBACK**: Commands to finalize or undo transactions.
- **Transaction Isolation Levels**: Different levels of isolation to control the visibility of uncommitted data.
- A **real-world example** of implementing a **bank transfer** operation in a banking system to ensure consistency and prevent errors.

Mastering transactions is crucial for handling critical data operations in real-world applications, ensuring that your data remains accurate and consistent, even in the event of failures. In the next chapter, we will explore more advanced SQL topics like

stored procedures, **triggers**, and **views** to further enhance your database management skills.

CHAPTER 12

INDEXES: IMPROVING QUERY PERFORMANCE

One of the most important aspects of working with large datasets in SQL is ensuring that queries are executed efficiently. **Indexes** are a powerful tool for improving query performance by allowing the database to quickly locate the rows that match a query's conditions. In this chapter, we will explore what indexes are, how they work, and how to use them effectively to optimize query performance.

We will also cover the **types of indexes**, including **primary key** and **unique indexes**, and demonstrate their use with a **real-world example** of indexing a product catalog for faster search performance.

---

1. What Are Indexes and How Do They Work?

An **index** in SQL is a database object that improves the speed of data retrieval operations on a table. Think of an index like an index in a book: it helps you quickly locate the data you're interested in without having to read through everything.

When a database table has an index on a column (or set of columns), it creates a data structure that allows the database engine to find the rows that match a query more efficiently, rather than scanning every row in the table.

How Indexes Work:

Indexes are typically implemented using **B-trees** (balanced trees) or **hashing**. These data structures store the values of indexed columns and provide quick access to the corresponding rows.

- **B-tree Indexes**: These are the most common type of index, and they allow for fast searching, insertion, and deletion of records.
- **Hash Indexes**: These are used for exact matching of values (i.e., equality checks) and are typically faster than B-trees for these operations, but they do not support range queries (e.g., greater than or less than).

Benefits of Using Indexes:

- **Faster Query Execution**: Indexes allow the database to find matching rows faster, significantly speeding up query performance.
- **Efficient Sorting and Filtering**: Indexes are especially useful for queries involving ORDER BY, GROUP BY, or WHERE clauses.

- **Reduced Disk I/O**: By using indexes, the database engine doesn't need to scan the entire table, reducing the number of disk reads required.

Downsides of Indexes:

- **Slower Data Modifications**: While indexes improve query performance, they can slow down **INSERT**, **UPDATE**, and **DELETE** operations because the index needs to be updated whenever data changes.
- **Increased Storage**: Indexes consume additional disk space, which can be significant for large tables with many indexes.

2. Creating and Dropping Indexes

2.1. Creating an Index

To create an index on a table, you use the CREATE INDEX statement. You can create an index on one or more columns in a table.

Basic Syntax:
sql

```
CREATE INDEX index_name
ON table_name (column1, column2, ...);
```

- `index_name`: The name of the index.
- `table_name`: The table where the index will be created.
- `column1, column2, ...`: The columns on which the index is created.

Example: Creating an Index on the Product Name

Suppose we have a `products` table, and we frequently query it using the `product_name` column. To create an index on product_name:

sql

```
CREATE INDEX idx_product_name
ON products (product_name);
```

This index will speed up searches and queries that filter by product_name.

2.2. Dropping an Index

If an index is no longer needed or if it is affecting performance (e.g., slowing down INSERT operations), you can drop the index using the DROP INDEX statement.

Syntax:
sql

```
DROP INDEX index_name;
```

- `index_name`: The name of the index to be dropped.

Example: Dropping the Product Name Index
sql

```
DROP INDEX idx_product_name;
```

This will remove the index on the `product_name` column from the `products` table.

---

3. Understanding Primary Key and Unique Indexes

Indexes are closely related to **primary keys** and **unique constraints**. When you define a primary key or a unique constraint, SQL automatically creates an index on that column or set of columns to enforce the uniqueness constraint and improve query performance.

3.1. Primary Key Indexes

A **primary key** uniquely identifies each row in a table. When you define a primary key on a column, SQL automatically creates a unique index on that column. A table can only have one primary key, but it can consist of multiple columns (known as a **composite primary key**).

143

Example: Defining a Primary Key on the Customer ID

sql

```sql
CREATE TABLE customers (
  customer_id INT PRIMARY KEY,
  first_name VARCHAR(50),
  last_name VARCHAR(50)
);
```

In this case, SQL automatically creates a unique index on customer_id, ensuring that each customer has a unique ID.

3.2. Unique Indexes

A **unique index** ensures that no two rows have the same value for a specified column or set of columns. Unlike primary keys, a table can have multiple unique indexes.

Example: Adding a Unique Index on Email

If you want to ensure that no two customers have the same email address, you can create a unique index on the email column:

sql

```sql
CREATE UNIQUE INDEX idx_email
ON customers (email);
```

This ensures that each email in the customers table is unique.

4. Real-World Example: Indexing a Product Catalog for Faster Search

Let's imagine you are building an e-commerce platform with a large **product catalog**. As the catalog grows, you need to ensure that searches for products are fast and efficient. Here's how indexing can help improve search performance:

Example Tables:

- **products**: Contains product details (e.g., `product_id`, `product_name`, `price`, `category`).
- **categories**: Contains category details (e.g., `category_id`, `category_name`).

Step 1: Identifying Searchable Columns

When users search for products, they typically look for product names, categories, and price ranges. These columns are good candidates for indexing.

Step 2: Creating Indexes on Searchable Columns

1. **Index on Product Name**: Since searches by product name are common, we'll create an index on `product_name`:

```
sql
```

```
CREATE INDEX idx_product_name
ON products (product_name);
```

2. **Index on Category**: If users often search for products within specific categories, we should create an index on `category_id`:

```
sql
```

```
CREATE INDEX idx_category_id
ON products (category_id);
```

3. **Index on Price Range**: If users filter products based on price, we can create an index on the `price` column:

```
sql
```

```
CREATE INDEX idx_price
ON products (price);
```

These indexes will significantly speed up queries that filter by `product_name`, `category_id`, or `price`.

Step 3: Optimizing a Search Query

Now, let's optimize a query that searches for products in a specific category and within a certain price range:

146

sql

```
SELECT product_name, price, category_id
FROM products
WHERE category_id = 3
AND price BETWEEN 50 AND 100;
```

With the indexes on `category_id` and `price`, this query will execute much faster, as the database can quickly locate the relevant rows using the indexes rather than scanning the entire `products` table.

Step 4: Dropping Unnecessary Indexes

If you notice that the `price` index is no longer used often in search queries, you can drop it to reduce the storage and performance overhead:

sql

```
DROP INDEX idx_price;
```

Conclusion

In this chapter, we explored the concept of **indexes** in SQL, which are essential for improving query performance by allowing the database to quickly locate and retrieve data. Key points we covered include:

- **What indexes are** and how they work to speed up query execution.

- **Creating and dropping indexes** using `CREATE INDEX` and `DROP INDEX`.

- **Primary key and unique indexes**, which are automatically created to enforce data integrity.

- A **real-world example** of indexing a product catalog to improve search performance.

Indexes are an essential part of database optimization, particularly when working with large datasets. In the next chapter, we will explore advanced topics such as **views**, **stored procedures**, and **triggers** to further enhance your SQL skills and database management practices.

CHAPTER 13

VIEWS: SIMPLIFYING COMPLEX QUERIES

In SQL, some queries can become extremely complex, especially when you need to join multiple tables, filter data, or apply aggregate functions. Writing such queries repeatedly can be tedious and error-prone. **Views** are an excellent way to simplify these queries by creating virtual tables that encapsulate complex logic.

A **view** is essentially a saved SQL query that can be treated as a table. Once created, a view can be queried just like a regular table, making it easier to work with complex data retrieval operations. In this chapter, we will explore the concept of views, how to create and drop them, and how they can simplify reporting and complex query management. We will also provide a **real-world example** of using views in an **HR system** to manage employee data.

1. What Are Views and How Do They Work?

A **view** in SQL is a **virtual table** that is defined by a query. It does not store data physically; instead, it stores the query that generates the data dynamically. When you query a view, SQL executes the underlying query and returns the result as if it were a table.

How Views Work:

- A view is created by writing a **SELECT** query.
- The **SELECT** query can join multiple tables, filter data, and apply aggregate functions.
- The result of the **SELECT** query is saved as a view, which can then be queried like a regular table.

Key Benefits of Using Views:

- **Simplifies Complex Queries**: You can write complex joins or filters once and save them in a view. Later, you can query the view without re-writing the same logic.
- **Improves Reusability**: Once created, views can be reused across multiple queries or reports.
- **Enhances Security**: Views can be used to expose only specific columns of a table, preventing direct access to sensitive data.
- **Abstraction**: Views provide a level of abstraction, allowing developers to work with simplified queries rather than dealing with complicated table structures.

2. Creating and Dropping Views

2.1. Creating a View

To create a view, you use the CREATE VIEW statement followed by the SELECT query that defines the view.

Basic Syntax:

sql

```
CREATE VIEW view_name AS
SELECT column1, column2, ...
FROM table_name
WHERE condition;
```

- view_name: The name of the view you want to create.
- SELECT column1, column2, ...: The query that defines the data in the view.
- FROM table_name: The table (or tables) from which to retrieve data.
- WHERE condition: The conditions used to filter the data.

Example: Creating a Simple View

Let's create a view called employee_summary that combines employee data from the employees table, showing only employees who are currently active:

sql

```
CREATE VIEW employee_summary AS
SELECT    employee_id,    first_name,    last_name,
job_title
FROM employees
WHERE status = 'Active';
```

This view will return only active employees when queried, simplifying future queries that need to retrieve this data.

2.2. Dropping a View

To remove a view from the database, you use the DROP VIEW statement.

Syntax:
sql

```
DROP VIEW view_name;
```

- view_name: The name of the view to be dropped.

Example: Dropping the employee_summary View
sql

```
DROP VIEW employee_summary;
```

This removes the employee_summary view from the database.

3. Using Views to Simplify Reporting

Views are often used to simplify complex queries, especially for reporting purposes. By creating views for common report queries, you can eliminate the need for users or developers to repeatedly write complex SQL.

Example: Simplifying a Sales Report

Suppose we have a sales database with the following tables:

- **orders**: Contains order information (`order_id`, `customer_id`, `order_date`, `total_amount`).
- **order_items**: Contains details about the products in each order (`order_id`, `product_id`, `quantity`).

A complex sales report might involve joining these two tables, aggregating sales by product, and applying various filters. Instead of writing this complex query every time you need the report, you can create a view that encapsulates the logic.

sql

```
CREATE VIEW sales_report AS
SELECT o.order_id, o.order_date, oi.product_id,
SUM(oi.quantity)          AS          total_quantity,
SUM(oi.quantity * p.price) AS total_sales
```

```
FROM orders o
JOIN order_items oi ON o.order_id = oi.order_id
JOIN products p ON oi.product_id = p.product_id
GROUP     BY     o.order_id,     o.order_date,
oi.product_id;
```

Now, you can retrieve the sales report by simply querying the view:

```
sql
```

```
SELECT * FROM sales_report;
```

This saves time and reduces errors, especially for recurring reports.

---

4. Real-World Example: Creating a View for Employee Data in an HR System

Let's consider an **HR system** where we store employee data in a table called `employees`. The `employees` table contains columns like `employee_id`, `first_name`, `last_name`, `job_title`, `salary`, `hire_date`, and `status`.

Suppose you need to create a report of all active employees who are in managerial positions, along with their salary information, for use in budget planning.

Step 1: Create the View

First, we will create a view that filters active employees who are managers and displays their first_name, last_name, job_title, and salary.

sql

```sql
CREATE VIEW active_managers AS
SELECT first_name, last_name, job_title, salary
FROM employees
WHERE status = 'Active' AND job_title LIKE
'%Manager%';
```

Now, we have a view called active_managers that contains all the necessary data about active managerial employees.

Step 2: Query the View

Next, you can simply query the view to get a list of active managers and their salary information:

sql

```sql
SELECT * FROM active_managers;
```

This query will return all active managers with their job titles and salaries, making it easy to analyze the managerial workforce for budgeting or planning purposes.

Step 3: Modify the View (if needed)

If, for example, we later decide to add the `hire_date` column to the report, we can modify the view:

sql

```
CREATE OR REPLACE VIEW active_managers AS
SELECT first_name, last_name, job_title, salary,
hire_date
FROM employees
WHERE status = 'Active' AND job_title LIKE
'%Manager%';
```

This command updates the `active_managers` view to include the `hire_date` of each manager.

Conclusion

In this chapter, we explored the concept of **views** in SQL and their role in simplifying complex queries. We covered:

- **What views are** and how they work to create virtual tables based on `SELECT` queries.
- How to **create and drop views** using the `CREATE VIEW` and `DROP VIEW` statements.

156

- How views can be used to **simplify reporting** by encapsulating complex query logic.
- A **real-world example** of creating a view for managing employee data in an HR system.

Views are an essential tool for improving the maintainability and readability of your queries, especially when working with complex data or generating recurring reports. In the next chapter, we will explore **stored procedures**, **triggers**, and **functions** to further extend the capabilities of SQL for automated and reusable operations.

CHAPTER 14

STORED PROCEDURES AND FUNCTIONS

In SQL, there are powerful features that allow you to encapsulate business logic, automate repetitive tasks, and improve performance: **Stored Procedures** and **Functions**. These are essential for building scalable and maintainable applications that interact with databases.

In this chapter, we will explore what **stored procedures** and **functions** are, how to create and execute them, and how they help encapsulate complex logic. We will also walk through a **real-world example** of writing a stored procedure for **inventory management**.

---

1. What Are Stored Procedures and Functions?

Both **stored procedures** and **functions** are sets of SQL statements that are stored in the database and can be executed multiple times. However, they serve different purposes and have distinct features:

158

1.1. Stored Procedures

A **stored procedure** is a precompiled set of SQL statements that can be executed as a single unit. You can think of it as a way to encapsulate complex SQL logic or business logic that needs to be executed multiple times. Stored procedures can accept parameters, execute multiple queries, and perform various tasks such as inserting, updating, or deleting data.

- Stored procedures do not return a value, but they can output results through **output parameters** or by performing tasks like modifying data.
- They are commonly used for tasks like data validation, complex reporting, and batch processing.

1.2. Functions

A **function** is similar to a stored procedure but with one key difference: a function always returns a value. Functions can be used in SELECT statements, in WHERE clauses, or anywhere that an expression is expected. They are primarily used to encapsulate a logic that returns a result, such as calculations or data transformations.

- Functions can return **scalar values** (e.g., integers, strings, dates) or **table values**.
- They are typically used for calculations, formatting, and data transformations.

2. Creating and Executing Stored Procedures

2.1. Creating a Stored Procedure

To create a stored procedure, you use the CREATE PROCEDURE statement. A stored procedure can take parameters, execute SQL queries, and return results to the caller.

Basic Syntax:

sql

```
CREATE PROCEDURE procedure_name (parameter1
datatype, parameter2 datatype, ...)
BEGIN
    SQL statements;
END;
```

- procedure_name: The name of the stored procedure.
- parameter1, parameter2, ...: Optional parameters that the procedure accepts.
- SQL statements: The SQL commands that are executed when the procedure is called.

Example: Creating a Stored Procedure for Adding New Employees

Let's say we need a stored procedure that adds a new employee to the employees table:

```sql
sql

CREATE PROCEDURE add_employee (
    IN p_first_name VARCHAR(50),
    IN p_last_name VARCHAR(50),
    IN p_email VARCHAR(100),
    IN p_job_title VARCHAR(50)
)
BEGIN
    INSERT    INTO    employees    (first_name,
last_name, email, job_title)
    VALUES (p_first_name, p_last_name, p_email,
p_job_title);
END;
```

This stored procedure takes four parameters: first_name, last_name, email, and job_title, and inserts a new employee into the employees table.

2.2. Executing a Stored Procedure

To execute the stored procedure, you use the CALL statement:

```sql
sql

CALL        add_employee('John',        'Doe',
'john.doe@example.com', 'Software Developer');
```

This will call the `add_employee` stored procedure and insert the new employee's details into the table.

2.3. Modifying a Stored Procedure

If you need to change the logic of a stored procedure, you can drop and recreate it:

sql

```
DROP PROCEDURE IF EXISTS add_employee;

CREATE PROCEDURE add_employee (
    IN p_first_name VARCHAR(50),
    IN p_last_name VARCHAR(50),
    IN p_email VARCHAR(100),
    IN p_job_title VARCHAR(50),
    IN p_salary DECIMAL(10,2)
)
BEGIN
    INSERT    INTO    employees    (first_name,
last_name, email, job_title, salary)
    VALUES (p_first_name, p_last_name, p_email,
p_job_title, p_salary);
END;
```

This version of the procedure adds a `salary` parameter and inserts it into the `employees` table.

3. Using Functions to Encapsulate Logic

3.1. Creating a Function

To create a function, you use the `CREATE FUNCTION` statement. Functions must return a value and can be used in SQL expressions.

Basic Syntax:
sql

```
CREATE FUNCTION function_name (parameter1
datatype, parameter2 datatype, ...)
RETURNS return_type
BEGIN
    -- SQL statements
    RETURN result;
END;
```

- `function_name`: The name of the function.
- `parameter1`, `parameter2`, ...: The input parameters for the function.
- `return_type`: The data type of the value the function returns.
- `result`: The value returned by the function.

Example: Creating a Function for Calculating Employee Bonus

Let's say we want a function that calculates an employee's bonus based on their salary. If their salary is above $50,000, the bonus is 10%, otherwise it is 5%.

sql

```sql
CREATE    FUNCTION    calculate_bonus    (p_salary
DECIMAL(10,2))
RETURNS DECIMAL(10,2)
BEGIN
    DECLARE bonus DECIMAL(10,2);

    IF p_salary > 50000 THEN
        SET bonus = p_salary * 0.10;
    ELSE
        SET bonus = p_salary * 0.05;
    END IF;

    RETURN bonus;
END;
```

This function takes p_salary as an input parameter, calculates the bonus based on the salary, and returns the result.

3.2. Using a Function in a Query

Once created, you can use the function in queries, just like any other expression:

sql

```
SELECT    first_name,    last_name,    salary,
calculate_bonus(salary) AS bonus
FROM employees;
```

This query will return each employee's name, salary, and the calculated bonus.

---

4. Real-World Example: Writing a Stored Procedure for Inventory Management

Let's consider an **inventory management** system where we need to update the stock quantity of products when an order is placed. We want to create a stored procedure that performs the following actions:

1. **Update the stock quantity** of the product.
2. **Insert an order record** into the orders table.

Step 1: Define the Inventory and Orders Tables

For this example, we have two tables:

- **products**: Contains `product_id`, `product_name`, and `stock_quantity`.
- **orders**: Contains `order_id`, `product_id`, `quantity`, and `order_date`.

Step 2: Creating the Stored Procedure

The stored procedure will take the `product_id` and `quantity` as input parameters, update the `stock_quantity` in the `products` table, and insert a record into the `orders` table.

sql

```
CREATE PROCEDURE place_order (
    IN p_product_id INT,
    IN p_quantity INT
)
BEGIN
    -- Check if there is enough stock
    DECLARE stock INT;

    SELECT stock_quantity INTO stock
    FROM products
    WHERE product_id = p_product_id;

    IF stock >= p_quantity THEN
        -- Update stock quantity
        UPDATE products
```

```
        SET  stock_quantity = stock_quantity -
p_quantity
        WHERE product_id = p_product_id;

        -- Insert order record
        INSERT    INTO    orders    (product_id,
quantity, order_date)
        VALUES    (p_product_id,    p_quantity,
NOW());

    ELSE
        -- Raise an error if not enough stock
        SIGNAL SQLSTATE '45000' SET MESSAGE_TEXT
= 'Not enough stock available.';
    END IF;
END;
```

Step 3: Executing the Stored Procedure

To place an order for a product, we can execute the stored procedure:

sql

```
CALL place_order(101, 3);
```

This will reduce the stock of the product with `product_id` 101 by 3 and insert a new record into the `orders` table.

Step 4: Handling Insufficient Stock

If the stock is insufficient (for example, if there are only 2 units in stock but the order is for 3), the stored procedure will raise an error, preventing the order from being placed:

sql

```
CALL place_order(101, 3);
```

If there are fewer than 3 units in stock, the error message Not enough stock available. will be shown, and no changes will be made to the products or orders tables.

Conclusion

In this chapter, we explored the concept of **stored procedures** and **functions** in SQL. Key points covered include:

- **Stored Procedures**: Precompiled SQL queries that can accept parameters and perform actions like data modification or transaction management.
- **Functions**: SQL logic that returns a value and can be used in expressions.
- **Real-World Example**: We demonstrated how to write a stored procedure for inventory management in a retail

system, showing how to update stock quantities and handle order placement.

Mastering stored procedures and functions is essential for building scalable, maintainable, and efficient database applications. In the next chapter, we will explore **triggers**, which are another powerful feature for automating tasks in the database based on events such as inserts, updates, or deletes.

CHAPTER 15

TRIGGERS: AUTOMATING ACTIONS IN THE DATABASE

In SQL, automating tasks in response to certain events is an essential feature for many applications, especially when ensuring data integrity, enforcing business rules, or auditing changes. This is where **triggers** come in. **Triggers** allow you to automatically execute certain actions in the database in response to specific events like **INSERT**, **UPDATE**, or **DELETE** operations.

In this chapter, we will explore **what triggers are**, **how they work**, and how to use them for various tasks, including **data validation** and **auditing**. We'll also work through a **real-world example** of logging changes to sensitive data in a healthcare system to demonstrate the power of triggers in automating database actions.

1. What Are Triggers and How Do They Work?

A **trigger** is a special kind of stored procedure that automatically executes or "fires" in response to specific events on a particular table or view. A trigger is associated with a table and can be set to execute **before** or **after** an `INSERT`, `UPDATE`, or `DELETE` operation.

How Triggers Work:

- Triggers are executed automatically in response to changes in data.
- You can set triggers to run **before** or **after** a data modification, depending on the need.
- A trigger can be used to enforce business rules, update other tables, or log changes, making it a valuable tool for maintaining data integrity.

Types of Triggers:

- **BEFORE Trigger**: Executes before the operation (INSERT, UPDATE, DELETE) is performed. It's typically used for data validation or modification before the operation happens.
- **AFTER Trigger**: Executes after the operation has been performed. It is often used for auditing, logging, or updating related tables.
- **INSTEAD OF Trigger**: Executes in place of the operation (instead of an INSERT, UPDATE, or DELETE). This is commonly used in views.

2. Creating and Managing Triggers

2.1. Creating a Trigger

To create a trigger, you use the CREATE TRIGGER statement. The syntax depends on the type of trigger and the event it responds to.

Basic Syntax for a Trigger:

sql

```
CREATE TRIGGER trigger_name
BEFORE/AFTER INSERT/UPDATE/DELETE
ON table_name
FOR EACH ROW
BEGIN
    -- SQL statements to execute
END;
```

- trigger_name: The name of the trigger.
- BEFORE/AFTER: Specifies whether the trigger should fire before or after the event.
- INSERT/UPDATE/DELETE: The event that triggers the action.
- table_name: The table that the trigger is associated with.
- FOR EACH ROW: Specifies that the trigger will operate on each row affected by the event.
- The trigger body (between BEGIN and END) contains the SQL logic to execute when the trigger is fired.

172

Example: Creating an AFTER INSERT Trigger

Let's create a trigger that automatically logs new employee records when they are added to the `employees` table. We will log the employee's name and the date of insertion into an `audit_log` table.

sql

```
CREATE TRIGGER log_employee_insertion
AFTER INSERT
ON employees
FOR EACH ROW
BEGIN
    INSERT    INTO    audit_log    (action_type,
table_name, record_id, action_date)
    VALUES          ('INSERT',          'employees',
NEW.employee_id, NOW());
END;
```

In this example:

- The trigger `log_employee_insertion` fires **after** a new row is inserted into the `employees` table.
- The `NEW` keyword is used to reference the newly inserted row's values (such as `NEW.employee_id`).

173

- The trigger inserts a record into the `audit_log` table, logging the action type (`INSERT`), the table name, the record ID (`employee_id`), and the timestamp (`NOW()`).

2.2. Dropping a Trigger

If you no longer need a trigger, you can drop it using the `DROP TRIGGER` statement.

```sql
sql
```

```sql
DROP TRIGGER IF EXISTS log_employee_insertion;
```

This removes the `log_employee_insertion` trigger from the database.

3. Using Triggers for Data Validation and Auditing

Triggers are often used for two key tasks in database systems: **data validation** and **auditing**.

3.1. Data Validation

Triggers can be used to validate data before it's inserted or updated. For example, you might want to ensure that certain values fall within acceptable ranges or that they meet specific business rules.

Example: Validating Age Before Inserting Customer Data

Let's say we have a `customers` table, and we want to ensure that the customer's `age` is between 18 and 100. We can use a `BEFORE INSERT` trigger to validate the age before inserting a new record.

sql

```
CREATE TRIGGER validate_customer_age
BEFORE INSERT
ON customers
FOR EACH ROW
BEGIN
    IF NEW.age < 18 OR NEW.age > 100 THEN
        SIGNAL SQLSTATE '45000'
        SET MESSAGE_TEXT = 'Age must be between
18 and 100';
    END IF;
END;
```

In this example:

- The trigger `validate_customer_age` checks the `age` column of the new row before it is inserted into the `customers` table.
- If the `age` is not within the allowed range, the trigger raises an error with the message "Age must be between 18 and 100."

3.2. Auditing Changes

Triggers are commonly used for **auditing**, which involves tracking changes to data over time. This is especially important for applications where data integrity and accountability are critical.

Example: Auditing Changes to Employee Salaries

Let's say we want to track any updates to the `salary` field in the `employees` table. We can create an `AFTER UPDATE` trigger that logs the changes in a separate `salary_audit` table.

sql

```
CREATE TRIGGER audit_salary_changes
AFTER UPDATE
ON employees
FOR EACH ROW
BEGIN
    IF OLD.salary <> NEW.salary THEN
        INSERT INTO salary_audit (employee_id,
old_salary, new_salary, change_date)
        VALUES (NEW.employee_id, OLD.salary,
NEW.salary, NOW());
    END IF;
END;
```

In this example:

- The trigger `audit_salary_changes` fires after an update to the `employees` table.
- It checks whether the `salary` has changed by comparing the old and new values (`OLD.salary` and `NEW.salary`).
- If the salary has changed, the trigger inserts a record into the `salary_audit` table, which logs the `employee_id`, the old salary, the new salary, and the date of the change.

This allows you to maintain a history of salary changes for auditing purposes.

4. Real-World Example: Logging Changes to Sensitive Data in a Healthcare System

In a healthcare system, it's crucial to track any changes to sensitive patient data. Let's say we have a `patients` table that stores information about patients, including their `patient_id`, `first_name`, `last_name`, and `medical_record`.

To ensure the integrity of this data, we want to log any changes made to the `medical_record` column in a separate `audit_log` table. This can be accomplished using a trigger.

Step 1: Define the Tables

- **patients**: Contains patient information, including `medical_record`.
- **audit_log**: Logs changes to sensitive data, such as `patient_id`, `changed_column`, `old_value`, `new_value`, and `change_date`.

Step 2: Create the Trigger

We create an `AFTER UPDATE` trigger that logs changes to the `medical_record` column:

sql

```
CREATE TRIGGER log_medical_record_changes
AFTER UPDATE
ON patients
FOR EACH ROW
BEGIN
    IF OLD.medical_record <> NEW.medical_record
THEN
        INSERT INTO audit_log (patient_id,
changed_column, old_value, new_value,
change_date)
        VALUES (NEW.patient_id,
'medical_record', OLD.medical_record,
NEW.medical_record, NOW());
    END IF;
```

```
END;
```

In this example:

- The trigger `log_medical_record_changes` is fired **after** an update to the `patients` table.
- It checks whether the `medical_record` has been modified by comparing the old and new values (`OLD.medical_record` and `NEW.medical_record`).
- If the `medical_record` has changed, the trigger logs the change in the `audit_log` table, including the patient's ID, the column name (`medical_record`), the old value, the new value, and the timestamp of the change.

Step 3: Executing the Update

Now, whenever the `medical_record` of a patient is updated, the trigger will automatically log the change in the `audit_log` table:

sql

```sql
UPDATE patients
SET medical_record = 'New medical condition diagnosed'
WHERE patient_id = 1;
```

This update will trigger the logging action, and the change will be stored in the `audit_log` table.

Conclusion

In this chapter, we discussed **triggers** and their role in automating database actions in response to specific events. Key topics included:

- **What triggers are** and how they work to automate actions in response to data modifications.
- **Creating and managing triggers** using the `CREATE TRIGGER` and `DROP TRIGGER` statements.
- **Using triggers for data validation** and **auditing** to ensure data integrity and track changes.
- A **real-world example** of using triggers to log changes to sensitive data in a healthcare system.

Triggers are a powerful tool for automating complex operations and maintaining data consistency in the database. In the next chapter, we will explore more advanced SQL techniques like **window functions**, **common table expressions (CTEs)**, and **recursive queries**.

CHAPTER 16

USER-DEFINED TYPES AND TABLES

In SQL, the ability to extend the database schema with custom data types and tables is an essential feature that allows for more complex and flexible data management. By using **user-defined types** and **user-defined tables**, you can design a more efficient and organized data model that fits your specific application needs.

In this chapter, we will explore how to create and use **user-defined types** (UDTs) and **user-defined tables** in SQL. We'll discuss how custom data types can help represent complex structures in the database, and show how to apply these concepts through a **real-world example** involving address information.

1. What Are User-Defined Types (UDTs)?

A **user-defined type (UDT)** is a data type that you can define yourself, rather than using one of the built-in SQL types like INT, VARCHAR, or DATE. UDTs allow you to create more complex data structures, such as composite types or types based on existing data types, tailored to your specific requirements.

181

Types of User-Defined Types:

- **User-Defined Scalar Types**: These are new atomic types that extend the built-in data types.

- **User-Defined Composite Types**: These are types that group together multiple values, potentially of different types, into a single entity. For example, an address can be defined as a composite type with street, city, and postal code fields.

- **User-Defined Enumerated Types**: These types allow you to define a list of possible values, often used for representing status, categories, or types.

User-defined types allow you to model real-world concepts more accurately and with better structure. They help make your database schema more intuitive and maintainable.

---

2. Creating Custom Data Types

2.1. Creating a Simple User-Defined Type

To create a **user-defined type**, you use the `CREATE TYPE` statement. In this example, let's define a custom type that represents a `full_name` consisting of a `first_name` and `last_name`.

Basic Syntax:

sql

```
CREATE TYPE full_name AS (
    first_name VARCHAR(50),
    last_name VARCHAR(50)
);
```

- **CREATE TYPE**: The command used to define a new type.
- **full_name**: The name of the custom type.
- **first_name and last_name**: The fields that make up the custom type.

Now, we have a custom data type `full_name` that can be used to store two pieces of information (first name and last name) together.

2.2. Using a User-Defined Type in a Table

Once the custom data type is created, you can use it in your tables like any other data type.

sql

```
CREATE TABLE employees (
    employee_id INT PRIMARY KEY,
    name full_name,
    hire_date DATE
);
```

In this example:

- The `employees` table contains an `employee_id`, a name field of type `full_name`, and a `hire_date`.
- The `name` field uses the custom `full_name` type to store both the first and last names together.

2.3. Inserting Data into Tables with UDTs

You can insert data into a table with a user-defined type like this:

sql

```
INSERT    INTO    employees   (employee_id,   name,
hire_date)
VALUES (1, ('John', 'Doe'), '2023-01-01');
```

In this query:

- The `name` field is populated with the custom type (`'John'`, `'Doe'`).

---

3. Using User-Defined Tables for More Complex Data Structures

3.1. What Are User-Defined Tables?

A **user-defined table** allows you to define a table type that can be used to store multiple rows of data. This is particularly useful

184

when you need to pass complex data structures as parameters to stored procedures or functions, or when you want to model more complex entities with multiple columns.

3.2. Creating a User-Defined Table Type

To create a user-defined table, you can use the CREATE TYPE statement with the AS TABLE clause. This allows you to define a table-like structure that can be used in a function or procedure.

Basic Syntax:
sql

```
CREATE TYPE address_type AS TABLE (
    street VARCHAR(100),
    city VARCHAR(50),
    postal_code VARCHAR(20),
    country VARCHAR(50)
);
```

- **CREATE TYPE**: The command to define a new type.
- **address_type**: The name of the custom table type.
- **Columns**: The fields that make up the custom table, such as street, city, postal_code, and country.

This creates a new table type called address_type with four columns, which can be used in stored procedures or functions.

3.3. Using a User-Defined Table Type in a Procedure

You can pass user-defined table types to a stored procedure or function. Here's how you can create a procedure that accepts a list of addresses (of type `address_type`):

sql

```
CREATE    PROCEDURE    insert_addresses    (IN
address_list address_type)
BEGIN
    INSERT   INTO   addresses   (street,   city,
postal_code, country)
    SELECT street, city, postal_code, country
    FROM address_list;
END;
```

In this example:

- The procedure `insert_addresses` accepts an input parameter of type `address_type`, which is a user-defined table.
- The procedure inserts all addresses from the provided list into the `addresses` table.

4. Real-World Example: Using Custom Types for Storing Address Information

Now, let's consider a **real-world example** where we need to store and manage **address information** for customers in an e-commerce system. The address information typically includes `street`, `city`, `postal_code`, and `country`, and it's common for customers to have multiple addresses.

We'll create a user-defined composite type for storing address details and then use it in a table to store multiple addresses for each customer.

Step 1: Define the Custom Address Type

We start by creating the `address_type` as a composite type:

sql

```sql
CREATE TYPE address_type AS (
    street VARCHAR(100),
    city VARCHAR(50),
    postal_code VARCHAR(20),
    country VARCHAR(50)
);
```

Step 2: Create the Customers Table with an Address Column

Now, we create a `customers` table with a `primary_address`
field that uses the custom `address_type`.

sql

```
CREATE TABLE customers (
    customer_id INT PRIMARY KEY,
    first_name VARCHAR(50),
    last_name VARCHAR(50),
    primary_address address_type
);
```

In this table:

- Each customer has a `primary_address` column that
  uses the `address_type` to store the customer's primary
  address.

Step 3: Inserting Data Using the Custom Address Type

Next, we can insert data into the `customers` table, including the
address information:

sql

```
INSERT INTO customers (customer_id, first_name,
last_name, primary_address)
```

```
VALUES (1, 'John', 'Doe', ('123 Main St', 'New
York', '10001', 'USA'));
```

This query inserts a new customer with their primary address. The address is stored as a composite type in the `primary_address` column.

Step 4: Querying Customers with Their Address Information

To retrieve a customer's information along with their address, you can simply query the table:

sql

```
SELECT customer_id, first_name, last_name,
primary_address
FROM customers
WHERE customer_id = 1;
```

The result will show the customer's name and their address in a structured format:

customer_id	first_name	last_name	primary_address
1	John	Doe	('123 Main St', 'New York', '10001', 'USA')

This query shows the customer's primary address in the form of the custom `address_type`.

Conclusion

In this chapter, we learned about **user-defined types (UDTs)** and **user-defined tables** in SQL, which allow you to create custom data structures and enhance the flexibility of your database design. Here are the key points we covered:

- **User-Defined Types (UDTs)** allow you to create complex, composite types that group related data together.
- **User-Defined Tables** provide a way to define a table structure that can be used as a parameter in stored procedures and functions.
- We explored a **real-world example** of creating a custom type for storing address information and using it in a table to manage customer data.

Custom types and tables allow for better organization and management of complex data in SQL, making it easier to work with real-world scenarios. In the next chapter, we will explore **advanced SQL features** like **window functions, recursive**

queries, and **CTEs (Common Table Expressions)** to further enhance your SQL querying capabilities.

CHAPTER 17

ADVANCED JOINS AND SUBQUERIES

In SQL, joins and subqueries are powerful tools for combining and retrieving data from multiple tables. While the basic concepts of **INNER JOIN**, **LEFT JOIN**, and **RIGHT JOIN** are widely used, there are advanced techniques that provide more flexibility and power when querying relational data. In this chapter, we'll explore **self joins**, **recursive queries**, and advanced **subquery techniques** to handle more complex data structures.

We'll also go through a **real-world example** of using **recursive queries** to retrieve an organizational hierarchy within a company.

1. Self Joins and Recursive Queries

1.1. What is a Self Join?

A **self join** is a join in which a table is joined with itself. It is often used when you have hierarchical or relational data within the same table. In a self join, the table is aliased (i.e., given different names) to avoid confusion between the two instances of the same table.

Example of a Self Join:

Consider an `employees` table with columns `employee_id`, `employee_name`, and `manager_id`. The `manager_id` column references the `employee_id` of the manager in the same table. To get a list of employees along with their manager's name, you would use a self join:

sql

```
SELECT     e.employee_name     AS     employee,
m.employee_name AS manager
FROM employees e
LEFT   JOIN   employees   m   ON   e.manager_id   =
m.employee_id;
```

- Here, the `employees` table is joined with itself using aliases (`e` for employees and `m` for managers).
- The `LEFT JOIN` ensures that we include employees even if they do not have a manager (e.g., top-level executives).

This query retrieves the name of each employee along with the name of their respective manager.

1.2. Recursive Queries

Recursive queries are used when querying hierarchical or tree-like data structures. A **recursive query** allows you to query data with a parent-child relationship within the same table. These types of queries are commonly used to represent organizational structures, folder hierarchies, or bill-of-materials systems.

Recursive queries typically use **Common Table Expressions (CTEs),** which can reference themselves.

---

2. Creating Recursive Queries

2.1. Common Table Expressions (CTEs)

A **CTE** is a temporary result set that you can reference within a SELECT, INSERT, UPDATE, or DELETE query. CTEs make it easier to manage complex queries, and they are particularly useful in recursive queries.

Basic Syntax for a Recursive CTE:
sql

```sql
WITH RECURSIVE cte_name AS (
    -- Base case: the non-recursive part of the
query
    SELECT column1, column2
    FROM table_name
    WHERE condition

    UNION ALL
```

```
    -- Recursive case: the recursive part of the
query
    SELECT t.column1, t.column2
    FROM table_name t
    INNER JOIN cte_name c ON t.some_column =
c.some_column
)
SELECT * FROM cte_name;
```

- **WITH RECURSIVE**: Specifies the recursive CTE.
- **Base case**: The initial query that provides the first set of rows for the recursion.
- **Recursive case**: A query that references the CTE itself to perform the recursion.
- **UNION ALL**: Combines the base case and recursive case.

2.2. Real-World Example: Recursive Query for Organizational Hierarchy in a Company

Let's say we have an employees table with columns employee_id, employee_name, and manager_id. The manager_id refers to the employee_id of an employee's manager. We want to query the entire organizational hierarchy, starting from a top-level manager and including all subordinates.

Step 1: Sample Employees Table

employee_id	employee_name	manager_id
1	John Smith	NULL
2	Sarah Brown	1
3	Emily Clark	1
4	James Davis	2
5	Lisa Johnson	2
6	Michael Lee	3

Here, John Smith is the top-level manager, and the manager_id references the employee_id of each employee's manager.

Step 2: Writing the Recursive Query

We will write a recursive query to list all employees in the company, starting from John Smith:

sql

```
WITH RECURSIVE org_hierarchy AS (
    -- Base case: Select the top-level manager
```

```
    SELECT        employee_id,        employee_name,
manager_id
    FROM employees
    WHERE manager_id IS NULL


    UNION ALL


    -- Recursive case: Select employees and their
subordinates
    SELECT    e.employee_id,    e.employee_name,
e.manager_id
    FROM employees e
    INNER JOIN org_hierarchy oh ON e.manager_id
= oh.employee_id
)
SELECT * FROM org_hierarchy;
```

Explanation:

1. **Base case**: Select the top-level manager (`manager_id IS NULL`), which in this case is `John Smith`.

2. **Recursive case**: Join the `employees` table with the `org_hierarchy` CTE to retrieve all employees whose `manager_id` matches an `employee_id` in the hierarchy. This process repeats for each level in the hierarchy.

3. **Result**: The query will return all employees, starting from `John Smith` and including their subordinates:

employee_id	employee_name	manager_id
1	John Smith	NULL
2	Sarah Brown	1
3	Emily Clark	1
4	James Davis	2
5	Lisa Johnson	2
6	Michael Lee	3

The query successfully returns the entire organizational hierarchy, starting from the top and recursively including each level of subordinates.

---

3. Advanced Subquery Techniques for Complex Data

Subqueries are queries nested inside other queries, and they can be a powerful way to extract and filter data. Advanced subquery techniques can simplify complex queries and improve readability. Below, we explore some advanced subquery techniques:

3.1. Correlated Subqueries

A **correlated subquery** is a subquery that references columns from the outer query. It is evaluated once for each row processed by the outer query.

Example: Correlated Subquery for Finding Employees Earning More Than Their Manager

Suppose we want to find employees who earn more than their managers. We can use a correlated subquery to compare an employee's salary with their manager's salary.

sql

```
SELECT e.employee_name, e.salary
FROM employees e
WHERE e.salary > (
    SELECT manager.salary
    FROM employees manager
    WHERE manager.employee_id = e.manager_id
);
```

In this query:

- The subquery references the `employee_id` of the outer query (`e.manager_id`), making it a correlated subquery.
- The query returns employees whose salary is greater than their manager's salary.

199

3.2. Subqueries in the SELECT Clause

You can also use subqueries in the `SELECT` clause to calculate derived columns.

Example: Calculating the Average Salary per Department

Assuming we have a `departments` table and an `employees` table, we can use a subquery in the `SELECT` clause to calculate the average salary per department.

sql

```sql
SELECT d.department_name,
       (SELECT AVG(e.salary) FROM employees e
WHERE e.department_id = d.department_id) AS
avg_salary
FROM departments d;
```

This query returns each department's name along with the average salary of its employees, calculated using a subquery.

Conclusion

In this chapter, we explored advanced techniques in SQL for handling complex data scenarios. Key points included:

- **Self Joins**: Using a table's self-referencing column to query hierarchical data within the same table.

- **Recursive Queries**: Using recursive Common Table Expressions (CTEs) to handle hierarchical data, such as retrieving an organizational structure.

- **Advanced Subquery Techniques**: Using correlated subqueries and subqueries in the SELECT clause to solve complex problems.

We also discussed a **real-world example** of using a recursive query to model an organizational hierarchy within a company.

Mastering these advanced techniques will allow you to tackle more complex data relationships and queries in your SQL work. In the next chapter, we will dive into **window functions** and explore how they can be used for advanced data analysis and reporting.

CHAPTER 18

DATA INTEGRITY: CONSTRAINTS AND VALIDATION

Data integrity is crucial to ensuring the accuracy and reliability of data in a database. **Constraints** are rules or conditions placed on data that help enforce data integrity. These rules prevent invalid data from being entered into a database and help maintain consistency across your data.

In this chapter, we'll cover various types of constraints, including **primary**, **foreign**, **unique**, and **check** constraints. We'll also discuss how to use these constraints to enforce data validation. Finally, we'll walk through a **real-world example** of enforcing data validation in an **online registration form**.

---

1. Defining Primary, Foreign, Unique, and Check Constraints

1.1. Primary Key Constraint

A **primary key** is used to uniquely identify each row in a table. It ensures that no two rows can have the same value for the primary key column(s). The primary key is always **unique** and **non-null**.

Example: Creating a Primary Key

When defining a table, you can specify the primary key using the PRIMARY KEY constraint:

sql

```
CREATE TABLE students (
    student_id INT PRIMARY KEY,
    first_name VARCHAR(50),
    last_name VARCHAR(50)
);
```

- In this example, the student_id column is the primary key, ensuring that each student has a unique ID.

1.2. Foreign Key Constraint

A **foreign key** is a column or group of columns in a table that links to the primary key of another table. The foreign key ensures referential integrity, meaning that a record in one table must correspond to an existing record in another table.

Example: Creating a Foreign Key

If you have an enrollments table that references the students table, you can define a foreign key as follows:

sql

```
CREATE TABLE enrollments (
    enrollment_id INT PRIMARY KEY,
    student_id INT,
    course_id INT,
    FOREIGN    KEY    (student_id)    REFERENCES
students(student_id)
);
```

- In this example, student_id in the enrollments table is a foreign key that references the student_id in the students table.
- The foreign key ensures that a student must exist in the students table before enrolling in a course.

1.3. Unique Constraint

A **unique constraint** ensures that all values in a column or group of columns are different from each other. Unlike a primary key, a column with a unique constraint can contain NULL values (if allowed).

Example: Creating a Unique Constraint

If you want to ensure that each student's email address is unique, you can create a unique constraint on the email column:

sql

```
CREATE TABLE students (
    student_id INT PRIMARY KEY,
    first_name VARCHAR(50),
    last_name VARCHAR(50),
    email VARCHAR(100) UNIQUE
);
```

- This query ensures that no two students can have the same email address.

1.4. Check Constraint

A **check constraint** allows you to enforce a rule that data in a column must meet certain conditions. For example, you can ensure that a column only contains values within a specific range, such as ages greater than 18.

Example: Creating a Check Constraint

If you want to ensure that the age column in the students table only contains values greater than or equal to 18, you can define a check constraint:

sql

```
CREATE TABLE students (
    student_id INT PRIMARY KEY,
    first_name VARCHAR(50),
    last_name VARCHAR(50),
```

```
age INT CHECK (age >= 18)
);
```

- This constraint ensures that no student can be added to the table with an age less than 18.

---

2. Enforcing Data Integrity with Constraints

Constraints are essential for maintaining **data integrity**, which refers to the accuracy, consistency, and reliability of the data. By using constraints, you can ensure that the data adheres to business rules and prevents unwanted or incorrect entries.

2.1. Preventing Duplicate Data with Primary and Unique Keys

By defining **primary keys** and **unique keys**, you ensure that each row in your table has unique data. The primary key is automatically indexed, making searches for specific records faster. The unique constraint guarantees that no two rows will have the same value in the specified columns.

2.2. Ensuring Consistency with Foreign Keys

The **foreign key** constraint ensures referential integrity by enforcing relationships between tables. If you try to insert a value into a foreign key column that does not exist in the referenced table, SQL will raise an error. This helps maintain consistency and prevents orphaned records (records that reference non-existent rows).

2.3. Validating Data with Check Constraints

Check constraints help ensure that the data inserted into the table follows specific business rules. For instance, you can use check constraints to ensure valid data formats, enforce valid age ranges, or restrict the values of a column to specific options (e.g., "active" or "inactive" statuses).

By enforcing such constraints, you can ensure that only valid data is stored in the database, which helps prevent errors and inconsistencies in the application.

3. Real-World Example: Enforcing Data Validation in an Online Registration Form

Let's consider an **online registration form** for a web application that allows users to create accounts. The form collects data such as `username, email, password, date_of_birth,` and `status.`

We'll design a table for storing user data and apply appropriate constraints to enforce data validation.

Step 1: Designing the Users Table

We want to ensure:

- Each user has a unique `username` and `email`.
- The `email` must follow a valid format.
- The `password` must meet certain security requirements.
- The `status` can only be `active` or `inactive`.
- The `date_of_birth` must be a valid date (i.e., the user must be at least 18 years old).

Step 2: Creating the Users Table with Constraints

sql

```sql
CREATE TABLE users (
    user_id INT PRIMARY KEY,
    username VARCHAR(50) UNIQUE NOT NULL,
    email VARCHAR(100) UNIQUE NOT NULL,
    password VARCHAR(255) NOT NULL,
    date_of_birth DATE NOT NULL,
    status    VARCHAR(10)    CHECK    (status    IN
('active', 'inactive')),
    CONSTRAINT         chk_age         CHECK
(DATEDIFF(CURRENT_DATE, date_of_birth) / 365.25
>= 18)
);
```

In this design:

- **Primary Key**: The `user_id` column is the primary key.
- **Unique Constraints**: The `username` and `email` columns are marked with `UNIQUE` to prevent duplicates.
- **Check Constraints**: The `status` column is constrained to only allow the values `active` or `inactive`. Additionally, the `chk_age` constraint ensures that users must be at least 18 years old by calculating their age based on the `date_of_birth` column.

Step 3: Inserting Data into the Users Table

To insert a new user, you can use the following SQL statement:

sql

```
INSERT INTO users (user_id, username, email,
password, date_of_birth, status)
VALUES (1, 'john_doe', 'john.doe@example.com',
'hashed_password_here', '2000-01-01', 'active');
```

- The constraints will automatically enforce the rules when data is inserted:
  - o If the `username` or `email` already exists, an error will be raised.
  - o If the `status` is not `active` or `inactive`, an error will be raised.
  - o If the user is under 18 years old, an error will be raised.

209

Step 4: Error Handling

If someone tries to insert an invalid entry, such as a duplicate email or an age under 18, the SQL engine will automatically reject the operation. For example, inserting a user with an invalid age:

sql

```
INSERT INTO users (user_id, username, email,
password, date_of_birth, status)
VALUES (2, 'jane_doe', 'jane.doe@example.com',
'hashed_password_here',          '2010-05-20',
'inactive');
```

This will fail with an error due to the `chk_age` constraint, as the user is under 18.

Conclusion

In this chapter, we discussed the importance of **data integrity** and how **constraints** in SQL help enforce it. We explored:

- **Primary Key, Foreign Key, Unique, and Check constraints**, which allow you to maintain consistency, prevent duplicate data, and validate user input.

- How to **enforce data integrity** by using constraints to define business rules and ensure that only valid data is entered into your tables.
- A **real-world example** of enforcing data validation in an **online registration form** for a web application.

Using constraints properly is essential to ensure that your database remains clean, accurate, and reliable. In the next chapter, we will dive into **performance optimization techniques**, including **indexes** and **query tuning** to further enhance your database's performance.

CHAPTER 19

NORMALIZATION AND DENORMALIZATION

When designing a database, the way data is structured can significantly affect its performance, integrity, and scalability. Two key concepts in database design are **normalization** and **denormalization**. **Normalization** is the process of organizing data to minimize redundancy and dependency, while **denormalization** is the process of deliberately introducing redundancy for performance optimization.

In this chapter, we will cover the **process of normalization**, its various forms (1NF, 2NF, 3NF, BCNF), and explore when and why you might want to **denormalize** a database for performance. We will also work through a **real-world example** of normalizing a **sales order database**.

---

1. Understanding the Process of Normalization

Normalization is a multi-step process used to organize a relational database. The goal is to reduce redundancy, avoid undesirable characteristics like **update anomalies**, and improve data integrity.

This process involves dividing large tables into smaller, more manageable ones and defining relationships between them.

There are several **normal forms (NF)**, each serving a different level of data normalization. We will discuss the most common forms: **First Normal Form (1NF), Second Normal Form (2NF), Third Normal Form (3NF),** and **Boyce-Codd Normal Form (BCNF)**.

1.1. First Normal Form (1NF)

A table is in **First Normal Form (1NF)** if:

- Every column contains atomic (indivisible) values.
- Each column contains only a single value for each row (no repeating groups).
- All entries in a column must be of the same type.

In other words, **1NF** requires that a table has a **primary key** and that each column in the table contains unique, indivisible values.

Example of 1NF:

Consider a `customers` table where a customer can have multiple phone numbers:

customer_id	customer_name	phone_numbers
1	John Doe	(555) 123-4567, (555) 234-5678
2	Jane Smith	(555) 345-6789

In the above example, the `phone_numbers` column violates 1NF because it contains multiple values. To bring this into 1NF, we would separate each phone number into its own row:

customer_id	customer_name	phone_number
1	John Doe	(555) 123-4567
1	John Doe	(555) 234-5678
2	Jane Smith	(555) 345-6789

Now, the table is in 1NF because each column contains atomic values.

1.2. Second Normal Form (2NF)

A table is in **Second Normal Form (2NF)** if:

- It is in 1NF.

- There are no partial dependencies, meaning all non-key attributes are fully dependent on the **entire** primary key.

In simple terms, 2NF requires that there are no **partial dependencies**, i.e., each non-key attribute must depend on the entire primary key, not just part of it.

Example of 2NF:

Consider an `order_items` table where each row contains the `order_id`, `product_id`, `product_name`, and `quantity`:

order_id	product_id	product_name	quantity
1	101	Apple	10
1	102	Banana	5

In this example, the `product_name` depends only on `product_id`, not on the entire `order_id` and `product_id` combination. To bring this into 2NF, we would split this table into two tables: one for orders and another for products:

Orders Table:

order_id	product_id	quantity
1	101	10
1	102	5

Products Table:

product_id	product_name
101	Apple
102	Banana

Now, each non-key attribute (like `product_name`) depends entirely on the primary key (`product_id`).

1.3. Third Normal Form (3NF)

A table is in **Third Normal Form (3NF)** if:

- It is in 2NF.
- There are no transitive dependencies, meaning non-key attributes do not depend on other non-key attributes.

Transitive dependencies occur when one non-key attribute depends on another non-key attribute, which is not acceptable in 3NF.

Example of 3NF:

Consider a `students` table with columns `student_id`, `student_name`, `advisor_name`, and `advisor_phone`:

student_id	student_name	advisor_name	advisor_phone
1	Alice	Dr. Smith	(555) 111-2222
2	Bob	Dr. Brown	(555) 222-3333

Here, `advisor_phone` depends on `advisor_name`, which is a transitive dependency, as `advisor_name` is not a key attribute. To bring this table into 3NF, we should split it into two tables:

Students Table:

student_id	student_name	advisor_name
1	Alice	Dr. Smith
2	Bob	Dr. Brown

Advisors Table:

advisor_name	advisor_phone
Dr. Smith	(555) 111-2222
Dr. Brown	(555) 222-3333

Now, the `advisor_phone` depends only on the `advisor_name` (which is a key attribute), and the table is in 3NF.

1.4. Boyce-Codd Normal Form (BCNF)

A table is in **Boyce-Codd Normal Form (BCNF)** if:

- It is in 3NF.
- For every **non-trivial functional dependency**, the left-hand side is a **superkey**.

In other words, BCNF resolves situations where a non-key attribute is functionally dependent on a part of a composite key or on another non-key attribute.

---

2. When to Denormalize for Performance

While normalization improves data integrity and reduces redundancy, it can sometimes make queries slower due to the need for complex joins across multiple tables. This is where **denormalization** comes into play.

2.1. Why Denormalize?

Denormalization is the process of combining tables that have been normalized, introducing some level of redundancy back into the database, for the sake of improving query performance.

- **Faster Queries**: By denormalizing data, you reduce the number of joins needed for complex queries, which can speed up retrieval times.
- **Simpler Queries**: Denormalized structures may result in simpler queries, making it easier to retrieve data without the need for joins.

2.2. When to Denormalize

Denormalization should be used sparingly and only when:

- You have performance issues due to excessive joins.
- The database workload involves heavy read operations and few updates.
- The performance gain outweighs the increased storage costs and potential inconsistencies.

Example of Denormalization:

Consider a denormalized version of the **sales orders** data. We might combine information from `orders`, `order_items`, and `products` into a single table to reduce the number of joins required in frequently executed reports.

---

3. Real-World Example: Normalizing a Sales Order Database

Let's consider a sales order system with the following information:

- **orders** table: Contains order details.
- **order_items** table: Contains products for each order.
- **products** table: Contains product details.

Step 1: Normalized Sales Order Database

In the normalized database, we split the information into multiple tables to reduce redundancy:

Orders Table:

order_id	order_date	customer_id
1	2023-01-01	1001

order_id	order_date	customer_id
2	2023-01-02	1002

Order_Items Table:

order_item_id	order_id	product_id	quantity	price
1	1	101	2	20.00
2	1	102	1	15.00
3	2	101	3	20.00

Products Table:

product_id	product_name	category
101	Apple	Fruit
102	Banana	Fruit

This setup eliminates data redundancy, ensuring that each piece of information is stored in only one place, but it may require multiple joins to retrieve all relevant information.

Step 2: Denormalized Sales Order Database

In a denormalized version of the sales order system, we combine the data from the `orders`, `order_items`, and `products` tables into one table to avoid the need for complex joins in frequently accessed reports:

Sales_Order_View:

order_id	order_date	customer_id	product_id	product_name	quantity	price
1	2023-01-01	1001	101	Apple	2	20.00
1	2023-01-01	1001	102	Banana	1	15.00
2	2023-01-02	1002	101	Apple	3	20.00

In this denormalized table:

- We store all information in a single table, which makes queries faster but introduces redundancy.
- If a product's price or name changes, we must update the information in multiple rows of the table, potentially leading to **update anomalies**.

Conclusion

In this chapter, we learned about the concepts of **normalization** and **denormalization** in SQL:

- **Normalization** helps to organize data efficiently by reducing redundancy, improving data integrity, and simplifying the database structure.
- **Denormalization** introduces some redundancy back into the system to improve performance, particularly when read-heavy operations are frequent.

We covered the different **normal forms (1NF, 2NF, 3NF, BCNF)** and how to apply them to ensure data integrity, and also looked at when **denormalization** is appropriate for performance reasons.

In the next chapter, we will explore **database indexing** techniques to further optimize query performance in large databases.

CHAPTER 20

SQL OPTIMIZATION AND QUERY PERFORMANCE

Efficient database queries are essential for building scalable applications. When dealing with large datasets, poorly optimized SQL queries can significantly slow down your application and negatively impact user experience. **SQL optimization** refers to techniques for improving the performance of your queries, making them run faster and more efficiently.

In this chapter, we'll cover essential strategies for optimizing SQL queries, including **analyzing query execution plans**, **indexing strategies**, and **avoiding common performance pitfalls**. We will also walk through a **real-world example** of optimizing search queries for an **e-commerce platform**.

---

1. Analyzing Query Execution Plans

1.1. What is a Query Execution Plan?

A **query execution plan** is a detailed breakdown of how the database engine executes a SQL query. The plan includes information about how the database accesses data (e.g., which indexes are used), how joins are performed, and the order in which operations are carried out.

Analyzing the execution plan is essential for identifying performance bottlenecks, such as full table scans, unnecessary joins, or missing indexes.

1.2. How to View Query Execution Plans

In most relational databases, you can view the query execution plan using special commands. Below are the commands for some common SQL databases:

- **MySQL**: `EXPLAIN SELECT query;`
- **PostgreSQL**: `EXPLAIN ANALYZE SELECT query;`
- **SQL Server**: Use the `Execution Plan` feature in SQL Server Management Studio (SSMS) or run `SET SHOWPLAN_ALL ON`.

1.3. Interpreting Execution Plans

A query execution plan typically includes:

- **Table Scans**: Indicates that the database is scanning the entire table. This can be slow, especially for large tables.
- **Index Usage**: Shows whether an index is being used to speed up data retrieval. If an index isn't used, you may want to create one.

- **Join Types**: Indicates the type of join being used (e.g., nested loop, merge join, hash join). Nested loops, for example, can be inefficient when joining large tables.
- **Sort Operations**: Indicates whether the database is sorting data, which can be expensive in terms of performance.

By studying the execution plan, you can identify which parts of the query need optimization.

---

2. Indexing Strategies for Faster Queries

Indexes are one of the most important tools for improving query performance. An index is a data structure that allows the database to quickly find and retrieve rows that match certain conditions. Properly designed indexes can drastically speed up query execution.

2.1. What Are Indexes?

An **index** is a database object that improves the speed of data retrieval operations on a table. Indexes are created on columns that are frequently used in search conditions (WHERE clauses), sorting (ORDER BY), or joins.

2.2. Types of Indexes

There are several types of indexes you can use depending on your query requirements:

- **Single-column indexes**: Created on a single column, useful when queries frequently search by that column.
- **Composite indexes**: Created on multiple columns, useful when queries filter or sort by multiple columns.
- **Unique indexes**: Enforce uniqueness on a column and help improve query performance when searching for unique values.
- **Full-text indexes**: Used for searching text-based data, allowing efficient searching of large text fields (like product descriptions in e-commerce platforms).

2.3. Indexing Strategy

1. **Use Indexes for Columns in WHERE Clauses**: If a query frequently filters data based on a column, create an index on that column.
2. **Create Composite Indexes for Multi-Column Queries**: If queries often filter on multiple columns, create a composite index that includes those columns.
3. **Avoid Over-Indexing**: While indexes improve read performance, they can degrade write performance. Each

insert, update, or delete operation requires the index to be updated.

4. **Consider the Order of Columns in Composite Indexes**: The order of columns in a composite index matters. If you frequently filter by `column1` and then `column2`, create an index on `(column1, column2)` instead of `(column2, column1)`.

Example of Creating an Index:

sql

```
CREATE INDEX idx_product_name ON products
(product_name);
```

This creates an index on the `product_name` column of the `products` table, which speeds up queries that search by `product_name`.

2.4. Monitoring Index Usage

After creating indexes, monitor how they are being used. Some queries may not use indexes if the database engine finds it more efficient to perform a full table scan. The query execution plan can help you identify which indexes are used and whether they are effective.

3. Avoiding Common Performance Pitfalls

While indexes are powerful tools, they are not the only factor in query performance. There are several common pitfalls to avoid:

3.1. Avoiding SELECT *

Using `SELECT` * retrieves all columns from a table, which can be inefficient, especially if you only need a subset of the columns.

sql

```
SELECT * FROM products;
```

This query retrieves all columns from the `products` table. Instead, always specify only the columns you need:

sql

```
SELECT product_name, price FROM products;
```

This query only retrieves the necessary columns (`product_name` and `price`), reducing data transfer and improving query performance.

3.2. Using Proper Joins

When performing joins, make sure you use the appropriate join type. For example, `INNER JOIN` is generally faster than `OUTER`

JOIN because it only retrieves matching rows, while OUTER JOIN includes unmatched rows as well.

Additionally, be mindful of the order in which joins are performed, and always join on indexed columns for optimal performance.

3.3. Avoiding Complex Subqueries

Subqueries, especially correlated subqueries, can be inefficient because they are executed once for each row in the outer query. Whenever possible, try to rewrite correlated subqueries as joins or use **Common Table Expressions (CTEs)** to simplify the query.

3.4. Using LIMIT for Large Queries

If you're working with large datasets and only need a subset of the results, always use the LIMIT clause (or its equivalent, depending on your database) to restrict the number of rows returned:

```sql

SELECT product_name FROM products ORDER BY price
LIMIT 10;
```

This query retrieves only the top 10 products by price, reducing the load on the server and improving performance.

4. Real-World Example: Optimizing Search Queries for an E-commerce Platform

Let's say we are building an **e-commerce platform** that allows customers to search for products. The `products` table contains columns like `product_id`, `product_name`, `category`, `price`, and `stock_quantity`. The search queries often filter products based on `category`, `price`, and `product_name`.

Step 1: Analyzing the Query Execution Plan

Let's analyze a simple search query that filters products by `category` and `price`:

sql

```sql
SELECT product_name, price, stock_quantity
FROM products
WHERE category = 'Electronics' AND price < 500;
```

By running EXPLAIN (in MySQL or PostgreSQL) or the equivalent in other databases, we can examine the query execution plan to check if the database engine is using indexes effectively. If the plan shows a **full table scan**, we may need to add an index on the `category` and `price` columns.

Step 2: Creating Indexes for Faster Searches

We can create a composite index on `category` and `price` to speed up this query:

sql

```
CREATE INDEX idx_category_price ON products
(category, price);
```

This composite index helps the database quickly locate products in the "Electronics" category with prices less than 500.

Step 3: Optimizing with a Full-Text Index for Product Names

If users also search for products by name (e.g., "smartphone"), we can create a **full-text index** on the `product_name` column for faster text-based searches:

sql

```
CREATE FULLTEXT INDEX idx_product_name ON
products (product_name);
```

This allows the database to efficiently search product names for keywords, improving search performance.

Step 4: Optimizing Joins and Other Queries

If the search queries also involve joins with other tables, like `orders`, we should ensure that the join conditions are based on indexed columns (e.g., `product_id`). Additionally, avoid using `SELECT *` and always limit the number of rows returned using `LIMIT` if appropriate.

Conclusion

In this chapter, we explored various techniques for **optimizing SQL queries** and improving query performance:

- **Analyzing query execution plans** helps you identify bottlenecks and inefficient operations.
- **Indexing strategies** (including single-column, composite, and full-text indexes) can drastically improve query speed.
- **Avoiding common performance pitfalls** such as `SELECT *`, unoptimized joins, and complex subqueries helps reduce query complexity and improve performance.
- We worked through a **real-world example** of optimizing search queries for an **e-commerce platform**, covering how to use indexes to improve the performance of frequently run queries.

Effective SQL optimization is key to ensuring that your applications remain fast and responsive as the volume of data grows. In the next chapter, we will dive into **database transactions**, focusing on maintaining consistency, isolation, and atomicity in your database operations.

CHAPTER 21

WORKING WITH COMPLEX DATA TYPES: JSON, XML, AND ARRAYS

In modern databases, handling complex data structures like **JSON, XML**, and **arrays** is increasingly important as applications store and process a variety of data types. SQL databases traditionally worked with flat, tabular data, but with the rise of NoSQL systems and the demand for more flexible data structures, relational databases have adapted to support more complex data types.

In this chapter, we will cover:

- **Storing and querying JSON data in SQL**.
- Using **SQL functions** for working with **JSON** and **XML** data.
- A **real-world example** of storing **user preferences** in JSON format in a **Content Management System (CMS)**.

1. Storing and Querying JSON Data in SQL

1.1. What is JSON?

JSON (JavaScript Object Notation) is a lightweight data format used to represent structured data based on key-value pairs. JSON is commonly used for APIs, configuration files, and web applications because of its simplicity and human-readability.

1.2. JSON Support in Relational Databases

Many modern relational databases, such as MySQL, PostgreSQL, and SQL Server, support **JSON** as a native data type. This allows you to store JSON data directly in your database and query it efficiently using SQL.

1.3. Storing JSON Data

You can store JSON data in a **column** with the JSON data type (available in databases like MySQL and PostgreSQL). Here's an example of creating a table with a JSON column:

sql

```
CREATE TABLE users (
    user_id INT PRIMARY KEY,
    name VARCHAR(100),
    preferences JSON
);
```

In this example:

- The `preferences` column is of type `JSON`, which can store a JSON object.

1.4. Inserting JSON Data

To insert JSON data into the `users` table, you can use the following query:

sql

```
INSERT INTO users (user_id, name, preferences)
VALUES (1, 'Alice', '{"theme": "dark",
"notifications": {"email": true, "sms":
false}}');
```

Here, the `preferences` column contains a JSON object that stores the user's settings, such as theme preferences and notification preferences.

1.5. Querying JSON Data

You can query the JSON data using the database's JSON-specific functions.

- **MySQL**:

To extract a value from a JSON object, you can use the JSON_EXTRACT function:

sql

```
SELECT              JSON_EXTRACT(preferences,
'$.theme') AS theme
FROM users
WHERE user_id = 1;
```

This will return the theme preference ("dark") for the user with user_id = 1.

- **PostgreSQL**:

PostgreSQL provides similar functions, such as ->> for extracting text from a JSON object:

sql

```
SELECT preferences->>'theme' AS theme
FROM users
WHERE user_id = 1;
```

2. Using SQL Functions for JSON and XML Data

2.1. SQL Functions for JSON Data

SQL databases offer various built-in functions to work with JSON data, allowing you to **extract**, **modify**, and **query** nested JSON objects and arrays.

MySQL and **PostgreSQL** have a variety of JSON functions, such as:

- **JSON_EXTRACT**: Extracts a value from a JSON object.
- **JSON_ARRAY**: Creates a JSON array.
- **JSON_OBJECT**: Creates a JSON object.
- **JSON_SET**: Updates an existing JSON object.
- **JSON_ARRAYAGG**: Aggregates values into a JSON array.

2.2. Example of Querying Nested JSON

Consider a `users` table where the `preferences` column contains a nested JSON object with notification preferences for email and SMS:

json

```json
{
  "theme": "dark",
  "notifications": {
    "email": true,
```

```
    "sms": false
  }
}
```

If you wanted to query for users who have email notifications enabled, you could use the following SQL query:

sql

```
SELECT user_id, name
FROM users
WHERE                    JSON_EXTRACT(preferences,
'$.notifications.email') = true;
```

This query extracts the `email` value from the nested `notifications` object and filters the users based on whether email notifications are enabled.

2.3. SQL Functions for XML Data

While JSON is increasingly popular, some applications still rely on **XML** data. SQL databases like MySQL and SQL Server also offer XML support.

In **SQL Server**, for example, you can use the `XML` data type and related functions to work with XML data:

- **XMLQUERY**: Executes an XPath query against XML data.
- **XMLTABLE**: Converts XML data into a relational format.

- **VALUE**: Extracts a value from XML.

For instance, if you have an `orders` table with an `order_details` column storing XML data, you could query the order's total price using XPath:

sql

```
SELECT                                    order_id,
order_details.value('(/order/total_price)[1]',
'DECIMAL(10,2)') AS total_price
FROM orders;
```

This query extracts the `total_price` from the XML stored in the `order_details` column.

---

3. Real-World Example: Storing User Preferences in JSON Format in a Content Management System

Let's consider a **Content Management System (CMS)** where users can personalize their experience by setting preferences such as **theme, notifications**, and **privacy settings**. These preferences can be stored in JSON format to provide flexibility and ease of use.

Step 1: Designing the Database Table

We will create a `users` table where the `preferences` column is a `JSON` type. This allows us to store structured data, such as theme preferences and notification settings, in a flexible format.

sql

```
CREATE TABLE users (
    user_id INT PRIMARY KEY,
    name VARCHAR(100),
    preferences JSON
);
```

Step 2: Storing User Preferences in JSON Format

Now, let's store some user preferences. For example, `Alice` wants a dark theme and email notifications enabled, while `Bob` prefers a light theme with SMS notifications.

sql

```
INSERT INTO users (user_id, name, preferences)
VALUES
(1, 'Alice', '{"theme": "dark", "notifications":
{"email": true, "sms": false}}'),
(2, 'Bob', '{"theme": "light", "notifications":
{"email": false, "sms": true}}');
```

This stores personalized preferences for Alice and Bob in the preferences column.

Step 3: Querying User Preferences

To retrieve the theme preference for all users, we can query the preferences column:

sql

```
SELECT user_id, name, JSON_EXTRACT(preferences,
'$.theme') AS theme
FROM users;
```

This query will return the theme for each user:

user_id	name	theme
1	Alice	dark
2	Bob	light

Step 4: Updating User Preferences

If Alice decides to switch to the light theme, we can update her preferences using JSON_SET:

sql

```
UPDATE users
```

243

```
SET     preferences    =    JSON_SET(preferences,
'$.theme', 'light')
WHERE user_id = 1;
```

This updates `Alice`'s theme to "light" in the `preferences` column.

Let's say we want to add privacy preferences, such as whether a user wants their data to be publicly visible. We can modify the `preferences` JSON structure and update the data accordingly.

```
sql
```

```
UPDATE users
SET     preferences    =    JSON_SET(preferences,
'$.privacy', '{"profile_visible": false}')
WHERE user_id = 1;
```

Now, Alice's `preferences` JSON might look like this:

```
json
```

```json
{
  "theme": "light",
  "notifications": {
    "email": true,
    "sms": false
  },
```

```
"privacy": {
  "profile_visible": false
}
}
```

Conclusion

In this chapter, we explored working with **complex data types** like **JSON, XML**, and **arrays** in SQL databases:

- **Storing and querying JSON**: We discussed how to store JSON data in relational databases and query it using SQL functions.
- **SQL functions for JSON and XML**: We covered the various functions available for manipulating JSON and XML data, making it easy to extract and modify structured data.
- **Real-world example**: We used **user preferences in a CMS** as a real-world example to demonstrate how to store, retrieve, and update JSON data in SQL.

Complex data types like JSON and XML offer flexibility and ease of use for modern web applications. In the next chapter, we will explore **database transactions** and how they ensure data consistency, isolation, and atomicity in multi-step operations.

CHAPTER 22

SQL FOR BIG DATA: HANDLING LARGE DATASETS

As applications grow and datasets become larger, handling **big data** in SQL databases can become challenging. Queries can slow down, and database performance can degrade if data is not managed efficiently. However, modern relational databases provide several strategies to handle large datasets effectively, including **partitioning tables**, **sharding**, and utilizing various performance optimizations.

In this chapter, we will cover techniques for efficiently handling **large tables** in SQL, including:

- **Partitioning tables** for performance optimization.
- **Sharding** databases to distribute data across multiple servers.
- A **real-world example** of querying large **sales datasets** for reporting.

1. Techniques for Efficiently Handling Large Tables

When working with large datasets, certain strategies can help improve query performance and prevent the database from becoming a bottleneck. Let's discuss some key techniques for handling large tables:

1.1. Indexing Large Tables

One of the first and most effective steps to improving query performance on large tables is to create **indexes**. Indexes help the database quickly locate rows based on the values in indexed columns, significantly speeding up retrieval times.

For large tables, creating **composite indexes** (indexes on multiple columns) can help when queries filter on multiple columns. For example, if you frequently query by `order_date` and `customer_id`, you can create a composite index:

sql

```
CREATE    INDEX    idx_order_date_customer_id    ON
orders (order_date, customer_id);
```

However, you should be careful with the number of indexes you create, as each index can slow down insert, update, and delete operations.

247

1.2. Optimizing Queries for Large Tables

Writing efficient queries is essential when working with large datasets. Some general tips for optimizing queries on large tables include:

- **Limit the Columns**: Use SELECT column_name instead of SELECT * to retrieve only the data you need.

  sql

  ```
  SELECT order_id, product_name, quantity
  FROM orders
  WHERE order_date > '2023-01-01';
  ```

- **Use WHERE Clauses Efficiently**: Filter rows as early as possible in the query to reduce the dataset size.

  sql

  ```
  SELECT order_id, product_name
  FROM orders
  WHERE order_date > '2023-01-01' AND quantity > 10;
  ```

- **Avoid Using Complex Joins on Large Tables**: Complex joins, especially without indexes, can degrade performance. Try to break up large queries into smaller, more manageable ones if possible.

1.3. Caching Query Results

For read-heavy operations, caching the results of common queries can drastically improve performance. Caching tools like **Redis** or **Memcached** can store the results of expensive queries in memory, reducing the load on the database for frequently run queries.

For example, if an e-commerce platform frequently queries for the most popular products, you could cache the result of this query and update it periodically.

1.4. Using Materialized Views

A **materialized view** is a database object that stores the result of a query. Unlike a regular view, which recalculates the result every time it is accessed, a materialized view is precomputed and stored, providing fast access to the data.

For example, for complex reporting queries, you might create a materialized view that aggregates sales data, allowing for faster access during reporting.

sql

```
CREATE MATERIALIZED VIEW sales_report AS
SELECT product_id, SUM(quantity) AS total_sales
FROM sales
GROUP BY product_id;
```

2. Partitioning Tables and Sharding

2.1. What is Partitioning?

Partitioning is a technique where a large table is divided into smaller, more manageable pieces, known as **partitions**. Partitioning is especially useful when dealing with time-series data (e.g., sales data over many years) or data that is logically divisible into distinct groups.

For example, you can partition a sales table by year, where each year's data is stored in a separate partition. This reduces the size of the table that needs to be scanned for queries, improving performance.

2.2. Partitioning Strategies

- **Range Partitioning**: Data is divided into ranges, typically based on date or numeric ranges.

sql

```
CREATE TABLE sales (
    sale_id INT,
    sale_date DATE,
    product_id INT,
    quantity INT
)
```

250

```
PARTITION BY RANGE (YEAR(sale_date)) (
    PARTITION  p2022  VALUES  LESS  THAN
(2023),
    PARTITION p2023 VALUES LESS THAN (2024)
);
```

- **List Partitioning**: Data is divided based on discrete values (e.g., product categories or regions).

sql

```
CREATE TABLE orders (
    order_id INT,
    product_id INT,
    quantity INT,
    region VARCHAR(50)
)
PARTITION BY LIST (region) (
    PARTITION p_east VALUES IN ('East'),
    PARTITION p_west VALUES IN ('West')
);
```

- **Hash Partitioning**: Data is divided evenly across a set number of partitions based on a hash function applied to one or more columns.

sql

```
CREATE TABLE customers (
    customer_id INT,
```

251

```
    name VARCHAR(100)
)
PARTITION BY HASH(customer_id)
PARTITIONS 4;
```

2.3. What is Sharding?

Sharding is a technique where a database is horizontally split into smaller, independent databases (shards). Each shard holds a subset of the data, typically by key range, user, or region. Sharding is commonly used in distributed databases to improve scalability and availability.

For example, a global e-commerce platform might store user data in different shards based on geographic regions (e.g., US, Europe, Asia), so queries related to customers from each region only access the relevant shard.

2.4. Sharding Strategies

- **Range-based Sharding**: Data is split into different shards based on a key range (e.g., user IDs 1–10000 in one shard, 10001–20000 in another).
- **Hash-based Sharding**: A hash function is applied to a key (e.g., `customer_id`), and the result determines which shard the data will reside in.
- **Directory-based Sharding**: A lookup table is used to determine which shard holds a particular record.

Sharding can be complex, as it requires managing multiple databases and distributing queries across them.

---

3. Real-World Example: Querying Large Sales Datasets for Reporting

Let's say we have a large e-commerce platform that stores sales transactions in a table called `sales`, with millions of rows. The company needs to generate monthly sales reports for different product categories.

Step 1: Designing the Sales Table

The `sales` table contains the following columns:

- `sale_id` (primary key)
- `sale_date` (date of the transaction)
- `product_id` (ID of the product sold)
- `category` (product category)
- `quantity` (quantity sold)
- `total_price` (total price of the transaction)

Step 2: Partitioning the Sales Table

We will partition the `sales` table by year, as sales data typically spans several years. This will speed up queries that filter by date range.

253

```
sql
```

```
CREATE TABLE sales (
    sale_id INT,
    sale_date DATE,
    product_id INT,
    category VARCHAR(50),
    quantity INT,
    total_price DECIMAL(10, 2)
)
PARTITION BY RANGE (YEAR(sale_date)) (
    PARTITION p2020 VALUES LESS THAN (2021),
    PARTITION p2021 VALUES LESS THAN (2022),
    PARTITION p2022 VALUES LESS THAN (2023)
);
```

Step 3: Querying Monthly Sales for a Specific Category

We want to generate a monthly sales report for the `Electronics` category. With partitioning in place, the query will only scan relevant partitions for the specified date range, improving performance.

```
sql
```

```
SELECT      MONTH(sale_date)      AS      month,
SUM(total_price) AS total_sales
FROM sales
WHERE category = 'Electronics' AND sale_date
BETWEEN '2022-01-01' AND '2022-12-31'
```

```
GROUP BY MONTH(sale_date);
```

This query retrieves the total sales for the `Electronics` category, broken down by month in 2022, and performs the query more efficiently by limiting the data to the relevant partitions.

Step 4: Sharding for Scalability

If the sales dataset continues to grow, we might want to implement **sharding**. For example, we could shard the `sales` data by region to distribute the load across multiple databases.

Each shard could hold sales data for a specific region:

- **Shard 1**: North America
- **Shard 2**: Europe
- **Shard 3**: Asia

Queries related to sales in North America would be directed to Shard 1, queries for Europe to Shard 2, and so on, improving scalability and query performance.

Conclusion

In this chapter, we explored techniques for efficiently handling large datasets in SQL:

- **Indexing** large tables and using **partitioning** to optimize query performance.
- **Sharding** databases to distribute data across multiple servers, improving scalability and availability.
- A **real-world example** of querying large sales datasets for reporting, with optimizations using partitioning and potentially sharding.

Handling big data efficiently in SQL databases requires a combination of techniques, including query optimization, indexing, partitioning, and sharding. In the next chapter, we will explore **advanced SQL functions** for analytical queries and reporting, including **window functions** and **common table expressions (CTEs)**.

CHAPTER 23

SECURITY BEST PRACTICES IN SQL

As the world increasingly relies on databases to store critical and sensitive information, **SQL security** has become an essential part of database management. Whether you're working with personal data, financial information, or customer details, ensuring the **integrity, confidentiality**, and **availability** of your data is paramount.

In this chapter, we will explore essential **SQL security best practices**, including:

- **Protecting sensitive data** with **encryption**.
- **Preventing SQL injection attacks**.
- **Managing user roles and permissions**.
- A **real-world example** of **securing financial data** in an **accounting system**.

1. Protecting Sensitive Data with Encryption

1.1. Why Encryption is Important

Encryption is the process of converting plaintext data into an unreadable format, which can only be reverted back to its original form using a decryption key. This ensures that even if unauthorized access occurs, the data remains secure and unreadable. In SQL, encryption helps protect **sensitive data** such as passwords, credit card information, and personal identification details.

1.2. Types of Encryption in SQL

- **Data-at-Rest Encryption**: This type of encryption protects data stored in the database. It ensures that data remains encrypted when stored in the database files or backups.
  - o **Example**: Using Transparent Data Encryption (TDE) in SQL Server or MySQL to encrypt the entire database.
- **Data-in-Transit Encryption**: This protects data when it is transmitted over a network. Secure connections, such as those using **SSL/TLS**, are used to encrypt the data being transferred between clients and the database server.
  - o **Example**: Enabling SSL for MySQL or PostgreSQL to ensure that all data transmitted between the database and the client is encrypted.

258

1.3. How to Implement Encryption

- **Encrypting Columns in SQL**: Many databases allow you to encrypt specific columns that hold sensitive data. For instance, if you store credit card numbers or personal identification numbers (PINs), encrypt these columns to prevent exposure.

Example: MySQL - Using AES Encryption

```sql
sql

CREATE TABLE users (
    user_id INT PRIMARY KEY,
    username VARCHAR(100),
    password VARBINARY(255)   --   store
encrypted passwords
);


-- Encrypt data before inserting
INSERT INTO users (user_id, username,
password)
VALUES          (1,           'john_doe',
AES_ENCRYPT('my_secure_password',
'encryption_key'));
```

In this example:

- o We use **AES_ENCRYPT** to encrypt the password before storing it in the database.
- o The `encryption_key` is a secret key used to encrypt and later decrypt the data.

- **Decryption**: To retrieve the original data, use the corresponding decryption function:

sql

```
SELECT    username,    AES_DECRYPT(password,
'encryption_key') AS decrypted_password
FROM users;
```

- **Encrypting Backups**: Ensure that backups are encrypted to protect data from unauthorized access. Many SQL database systems allow you to specify encryption during the backup process.

---

2. Preventing SQL Injection Attacks

2.1. What is SQL Injection?

SQL injection is a type of attack where an attacker executes malicious SQL queries through an input field in an application. If user inputs are not properly sanitized, an attacker can manipulate queries to gain unauthorized access, retrieve sensitive data, or perform harmful actions on the database.

2.2. How SQL Injection Works

SQL injection typically occurs when user input is directly included in an SQL query without proper validation or sanitization. For example:

sql

```
SELECT * FROM users WHERE username = '$username'
AND password = '$password';
```

If $username and $password are not properly sanitized, an attacker can enter malicious SQL code in these fields to bypass authentication or manipulate the query.

2.3. Preventing SQL Injection

To prevent SQL injection, follow these best practices:

- **Use Prepared Statements (Parameterized Queries)**: Prepared statements separate the SQL query from the data being passed in. The query structure is defined first, and the user input is supplied as parameters, ensuring it cannot interfere with the query logic.

  Example in MySQL (PHP):

  php

261

```
$stmt = $pdo->prepare('SELECT * FROM users
WHERE username = :username AND password =
:password');
$stmt->execute(['username' => $username,
'password' => $password]);
```

In this example, the user input ($username and $password) is safely passed as parameters and does not interfere with the query structure.

- **Use ORM (Object-Relational Mapping) Libraries**: ORMs automatically handle SQL query generation in a secure way. Using an ORM can help avoid direct SQL injection risks by abstracting raw SQL queries.
- **Input Validation and Sanitization**: Always validate and sanitize user inputs. For example, ensure that numeric fields only accept numbers, and string fields do not contain any unexpected SQL characters (e.g., ', --, ;).
- **Escape Special Characters**: If using dynamic SQL queries, ensure that special characters are properly escaped before being included in a query.

---

3. Managing User Roles and Permissions

3.1. Why User Roles and Permissions Matter

Properly managing user roles and permissions is critical to ensure that users only have access to the data and actions they are authorized to perform. This prevents unauthorized users from accessing sensitive data and ensures compliance with security policies.

3.2. Types of User Roles and Permissions

- **Admin Roles**: Admins typically have full access to the database, including the ability to add, modify, and delete data, manage user roles, and perform backups.
- **Read-Only Roles**: Users in this role can view data but cannot modify or delete records.
- **Custom Roles**: Custom roles can be created to suit the needs of different users, defining permissions for specific tables, columns, or actions.

3.3. Granting Permissions in SQL

SQL databases provide commands to grant specific permissions to users. Here's how you can grant different levels of access:

- **MySQL**:

```sql
sql

-- Grant SELECT permission to a user on a
specific table
GRANT SELECT ON database_name.table_name
TO 'username'@'host';
```

```
-- Grant full access to a user
GRANT ALL PRIVILEGES ON database_name.* TO
'username'@'host';
```

- **PostgreSQL**:

sql

```
-- Grant read-only permission to a user
GRANT SELECT ON table_name TO username;

-- Revoke all permissions
REVOKE ALL PRIVILEGES ON table_name FROM
username;
```

- **SQL Server**:

sql

```
-- Grant SELECT permission
GRANT SELECT ON table_name TO username;

-- Revoke permission
REVOKE SELECT ON table_name FROM username;
```

3.4. Principle of Least Privilege

Always follow the **principle of least privilege**: give users only the permissions they need to perform their job functions. This minimizes the risk of accidental or malicious data manipulation.

4. Real-World Example: Securing Financial Data in an Accounting System

In an **accounting system**, sensitive financial data must be protected to ensure the integrity and confidentiality of financial transactions. The system typically stores sensitive data such as **account numbers**, **transaction amounts**, **tax information**, and **employee salaries**.

Step 1: Encrypting Sensitive Data

The system stores financial data in the `transactions` table. To protect this data, we will encrypt sensitive columns, such as `account_number` and `transaction_amount`, before storing them in the database.

sql

```
CREATE TABLE transactions (
    transaction_id INT PRIMARY KEY,
    account_number VARBINARY(255),  -- Encrypted
account number
    transaction_amount   DECIMAL(10,   2),   --
Encrypted transaction amount
    transaction_date DATE
);
```

265

To insert an encrypted account number and transaction amount:

sql

```
-- Encrypt sensitive data before inserting
INSERT    INTO    transactions    (transaction_id,
account_number,                transaction_amount,
transaction_date)
VALUES
(1, AES_ENCRYPT('1234567890', 'encryption_key'),
AES_ENCRYPT('1000.00', 'encryption_key'), '2023-
03-01');
```

In this case, the `account_number` and `transaction_amount` columns are encrypted using **AES_ENCRYPT** before storing them in the database.

Step 2: Preventing SQL Injection

The application accepts user input for searching transactions. To prevent SQL injection, we use prepared statements:

php

```
// PHP code using prepared statements
$stmt = $pdo->prepare('SELECT * FROM transactions
WHERE account_number = :account_number');
$stmt->execute(['account_number'            =>
$account_number]);
```

This ensures that user input is safely passed into the SQL query, preventing SQL injection attacks.

Step 3: Managing User Roles and Permissions

We create specific roles to control access to sensitive financial data. For example, we grant **read-only access** to auditors and **full access** to administrators.

sql

```
-- Grant read-only access to auditors
GRANT    SELECT    ON    transactions    TO
'auditor'@'localhost';

-- Grant full access to administrators
GRANT    ALL    PRIVILEGES    ON    transactions    TO
'admin'@'localhost';
```

This ensures that only authorized users can view or modify sensitive financial information.

Conclusion

In this chapter, we discussed important **SQL security best practices** to protect sensitive data:

- **Encryption**: We explored how to encrypt sensitive data, both **at rest** and **in transit**, to ensure its confidentiality.

- **SQL Injection Prevention**: We covered how to prevent SQL injection by using **prepared statements** and validating user inputs.

- **User Roles and Permissions**: We discussed the importance of **role-based access control (RBAC)** to limit user access to only the necessary data and operations.

In the next chapter, we will explore **performance tuning** techniques for optimizing large databases, including **query optimization**, **indexing strategies**, and **partitioning**.

CHAPTER 24

BACKUP AND RECOVERY IN SQL

Ensuring the integrity and availability of data is one of the most critical aspects of database management. No matter how robust your database design or how well your system performs, **data loss** can still happen due to hardware failures, software bugs, accidental deletion, or security breaches. Therefore, **backup and recovery** strategies are essential for protecting your database and ensuring that you can restore it in the event of a disaster.

In this chapter, we will explore:

- **Creating backups** for disaster recovery.
- **Restoring data** from backups.
- A **real-world example** of **automating database backups** for a **cloud application**.

1. Creating Backups for Disaster Recovery

1.1. Why Backups Are Crucial

Backups are copies of your database that you can use to restore data if the original database becomes corrupted, deleted, or lost. A good backup strategy should ensure data integrity and minimize downtime in case of failure.

There are different types of backups, each suited to specific needs:

- **Full Backups**: A complete backup of the entire database. This is the most straightforward type of backup, but it can take a long time and require significant storage.
- **Incremental Backups**: Only changes made since the last backup are stored. This saves time and space, but it requires all previous backups to restore.
- **Differential Backups**: Backs up all changes made since the last full backup. While it takes more space than incremental backups, it is easier and faster to restore.

1.2. Creating Full Backups

Most relational database systems provide built-in commands for creating backups. Here's how to create backups in some common databases:

- **MySQL**:

Use `mysqldump` to create a backup of the entire database.

```bash
mysqldump -u username -p database_name > backup.sql
```

This command exports the `database_name` to a `.sql` file, which can be restored later.

- **PostgreSQL**:

Use `pg_dump` to back up a database:

```bash
bash
```

```
pg_dump -U username -F c -b -v -f backup_file database_name
```

The `-F c` option specifies a custom-format backup file.

- **SQL Server**:

Use the `BACKUP DATABASE` command:

```sql
sql
```

```
BACKUP DATABASE database_name TO DISK = 'C:\backups\database_name.bak';
```

1.3. Creating Incremental and Differential Backups

- **MySQL**: MySQL does not support native incremental backups, but you can use **binary logs** to capture changes since the last backup. By enabling **binary logging**, MySQL tracks all changes made to the database, and you can use the binary log to perform incremental backups.

271

```sql
sql
```

```sql
SHOW BINARY LOGS;
```

- **PostgreSQL**: PostgreSQL supports **point-in-time recovery (PITR)** through **WAL (Write-Ahead Logging)**. You can back up the WAL logs and archive them for incremental recovery.

```bash
bash
```

```bash
pg_basebackup -D /path/to/backup --wal-method=stream
```

- **SQL Server**: SQL Server supports both **differential** and **transaction log** backups.

```sql
sql
```

```sql
BACKUP DATABASE database_name TO DISK =
'C:\backups\database_name_diff.bak'  WITH
DIFFERENTIAL;
```

1.4. Automating Backups

For production systems, it's critical to automate backups to ensure they are performed regularly. You can schedule backup tasks using cron jobs (Linux), Task Scheduler (Windows), or built-in database tools.

Example: Scheduling a MySQL backup using `cron`:

```bash
bash
```

```
0 2 * * * mysqldump -u username -p password
database_name > /backups/database_name_$(date
+\%F).sql
```

This schedules a backup every day at 2 AM.

---

2. Restoring Data from Backups

2.1. Restoring Full Backups

Restoring a backup is the process of taking a previously backed-up database and replacing or rebuilding the original database. The method of restoration varies depending on the type of backup.

- **MySQL**:

    To restore from a `.sql` backup file created with `mysqldump`, use the following command:

    ```bash
    bash
    ```

    ```
    mysql -u username -p database_name <
    backup.sql
    ```

- **PostgreSQL**:

273

Use `pg_restore` to restore from a custom-format backup:

```bash
bash
```

```bash
pg_restore -U username -d database_name -v
backup_file
```

- **SQL Server**:

To restore a `.bak` backup file in SQL Server:

```sql
sql
```

```sql
RESTORE DATABASE database_name FROM DISK =
'C:\backups\database_name.bak';
```

2.2. Restoring Incremental and Differential Backups

When restoring from incremental or differential backups, you need to apply the most recent **full backup**, followed by any **incremental** or **differential backups**.

- **MySQL**: Restore the full backup first, then apply the binary logs for incremental changes.

```bash
bash
```

```bash
mysql -u username -p database_name <
full_backup.sql
```

```
mysql -u username -p < binlog1.sql
mysql -u username -p < binlog2.sql
```

- **PostgreSQL**: If using **PITR** with **WAL logs**, you can restore the full backup first, followed by replaying the archived WAL logs to bring the database up to the desired point in time.

- **SQL Server**: For differential backups, restore the full backup first, then apply the latest differential backup:

```sql
sql
```

```
RESTORE DATABASE database_name FROM DISK =
'C:\backups\full_backup.bak';
RESTORE DATABASE database_name FROM DISK =
'C:\backups\differential_backup.bak'  WITH
NORECOVERY;
```

2.3. Point-in-Time Recovery (PITR)

Point-in-time recovery allows you to restore your database to a specific moment, which is especially useful if the database has been corrupted or data was accidentally deleted.

- **MySQL**: Using binary logs, you can restore to a point-in-time by applying the logs up to a specific timestamp.

- **PostgreSQL**: Use `pg_restore` and restore from a full backup followed by the required WAL logs up to a specific timestamp.

275

- **SQL Server**: Use the RESTORE command with the STOPAT option to restore to a specific time.

---

3. Real-World Example: Automating Database Backups for a Cloud Application

In a cloud-based e-commerce application, the database stores sensitive data such as customer orders, payment details, and product inventory. To ensure business continuity and disaster recovery, we automate database backups and store them securely.

Step 1: Choose the Backup Strategy

We decide to use **daily full backups** combined with **incremental backups every 6 hours**. Full backups will be created at midnight, while incremental backups will capture changes made throughout the day.

Step 2: Automating Full Backups

We use cron jobs to schedule the full backup every day at midnight. The backup will be stored in a cloud storage service like **AWS S3** for redundancy.

bash

```
0 0 * * * mysqldump -u username -p password
database_name          |          gzip          >
/backups/database_name_$(date  +\%F).sql.gz  &&
aws    s3    cp    /backups/database_name_$(date
+\%F).sql.gz s3://ecommerce-backups/
```

Step 3: Automating Incremental Backups

Every 6 hours, we take an incremental backup, which stores only changes made since the last full backup.

bash

```
0 */6 * * * mysqldump -u username -p password --
incremental          database_name          >
/backups/incremental_$(date +\%F_%H).sql
```

We upload these incremental backups to AWS S3 as well.

bash

```
aws    s3    cp    /backups/incremental_$(date
+\%F_%H).sql s3://ecommerce-backups/incremental/
```

Step 4: Restoring Data

If the database becomes corrupted or lost, we can restore the last full backup, followed by the necessary incremental backups to bring the database up to date.

bash

277

```
mysql   -u   username   -p   database_name   <
/backups/database_name_2023-03-01.sql.gz
mysql   -u   username   -p   database_name   <
/backups/incremental/incremental_2023-03-
01_06.sql
```

This approach ensures that we can recover the data from the most recent backup, minimizing downtime and data loss.

Conclusion

In this chapter, we covered key concepts for **backup and recovery** in SQL databases:

- **Creating backups** using full, incremental, and differential strategies to ensure data can be restored after disasters.
- **Restoring data** from backups, including handling incremental backups and point-in-time recovery.
- A **real-world example** of automating database backups for a cloud-based e-commerce application, demonstrating best practices for backup scheduling and restoration.

Regularly backing up your database and testing the recovery process is essential for any production system. In the next chapter, we will delve into **database monitoring** and **performance tuning**, exploring tools and techniques to optimize your database's efficiency.

CHAPTER 25

DATABASE MAINTENANCE: KEEPING YOUR DATABASE HEALTHY

Maintaining a healthy database is critical to ensure that it operates efficiently, scales well over time, and can handle growing workloads without performance degradation. **Database maintenance** refers to the routine tasks necessary to ensure optimal performance, minimize downtime, and prevent data corruption.

In this chapter, we will discuss:

- **Regular database maintenance tasks** such as indexing and vacuuming.
- **Managing database growth** and performance over time.
- A **real-world example** of **maintaining a high-availability database cluster**.

1. Regular Database Maintenance Tasks

1.1. Indexing

Indexes are critical for improving database query performance. However, over time, indexes can become fragmented, and as data is inserted, updated, or deleted, the indexes might no longer be as efficient.

- **Rebuilding Indexes**: Rebuilding an index completely can help defragment it and improve performance. In **SQL Server**, you can rebuild indexes using the following command:

sql

```
ALTER INDEX ALL ON table_name REBUILD;
```

- **Reorganizing Indexes**: Reorganizing an index is a less resource-intensive operation than rebuilding and is usually done when index fragmentation is low to moderate.

sql

```
ALTER INDEX ALL ON table_name REORGANIZE;
```

- **Identifying Fragmentation**: Use the `sys.dm_db_index_physical_stats` function in

281

SQL Server or the `pg_stat_user_indexes` in **PostgreSQL** to check index fragmentation levels and decide whether to rebuild or reorganize.

1.2. Vacuuming

In databases like **PostgreSQL**, **vacuuming** is an essential task that helps recover space by cleaning up dead rows (rows that are no longer needed after an update or delete operation). Over time, dead tuples can accumulate and take up unnecessary space.

- **Vacuum Full**: This command reclaims space and defragments the database by compacting tables and indexes:

sql

```
VACUUM FULL;
```

- **Regular Vacuum**: Regular vacuuming helps to remove dead rows and maintain performance without doing the more intensive work of VACUUM FULL:

sql

```
VACUUM;
```

- **Autovacuum**: PostgreSQL has an **autovacuum** feature that runs vacuuming automatically in the background, but it's important to monitor it and adjust settings for optimal performance.

1.3. Updating Statistics

Databases use statistics about data distribution to optimize queries. As data changes, these statistics can become outdated, leading to poor query performance. Regularly updating statistics is important to ensure that the query planner makes optimal decisions.

- **SQL Server**: You can update statistics using:

```sql
UPDATE STATISTICS table_name;
```

- **PostgreSQL**: PostgreSQL automatically updates statistics, but you can manually refresh them with:

```sql
ANALYZE table_name;
```

1.4. Backup and Restore Testing

Regularly test your backup and restore processes to ensure data can be recovered in the event of a failure. Testing backups is a critical task that helps identify issues early and ensure disaster recovery processes are reliable.

- Schedule routine test restores from backups, especially for production databases.

---

2. Managing Database Growth and Performance Over Time

2.1. Handling Database Growth

As data accumulates, a database can grow large, impacting both storage and performance. Properly managing growth is key to avoiding performance issues and ensuring that the database remains manageable.

- **Archiving Old Data**: For systems that generate a large amount of data, such as transaction logs or historical records, you can archive old data periodically and store it in separate tables or databases. This reduces the volume of active data in the primary database.

  Example: Moving older transactions to an archive table:

  sql

```
INSERT INTO archived_transactions (SELECT
* FROM transactions WHERE transaction_date
< '2022-01-01');
DELETE FROM transactions WHERE
transaction_date < '2022-01-01';
```

- **Partitioning**: As discussed earlier, partitioning large tables can improve performance by dividing the data into smaller, manageable chunks based on key ranges, dates, or other attributes.

  o **Range Partitioning**: Partition a table based on a range of values (e.g., by year or month).

  o **List Partitioning**: Partition based on discrete values (e.g., product categories or geographic regions).

  o **Hash Partitioning**: Use a hash function to evenly distribute data across partitions.

- **Scaling Storage**: As the database grows, you may need to scale your storage infrastructure. This can be done by expanding your disk space or utilizing cloud-based solutions like **Amazon RDS** or **Azure SQL Database** for scalable storage.

2.2. Managing Query Performance Over Time

As your database grows, queries may slow down. It's important to regularly review the performance of your queries and optimize them.

- **Query Optimization**: Continuously monitor query performance using execution plans. Look for slow-running queries, and consider adding indexes, rewriting queries, or optimizing joins and subqueries.

o **Example**: Using the `EXPLAIN` statement in **PostgreSQL** or **MySQL** to analyze slow queries.

```sql
EXPLAIN ANALYZE SELECT * FROM sales WHERE
order_date > '2023-01-01';
```

- **Caching**: Implement **query result caching** to reduce database load for frequently executed queries. Tools like **Redis** or **Memcached** can store query results in memory for faster access.
- **Connection Pooling**: Use connection pooling to reduce the overhead of repeatedly opening and closing database connections. This improves the overall performance and reduces the load on the database server.

2.3. Monitoring and Alerts

To manage performance over time, it's essential to implement monitoring and alerting mechanisms. This will allow you to identify performance degradation early and take action before issues affect users.

- **Monitoring Tools**: Use database monitoring tools such as **Prometheus, Grafana,** or built-in solutions like **SQL Server Management Studio** or **pgAdmin** to monitor query performance, disk usage, CPU usage, and other key metrics.

- **Alerting**: Set up alerts to notify you when performance thresholds are breached, such as when the database is running low on disk space or when queries take longer than expected.

---

3. Real-World Example: Maintaining a High-Availability Database Cluster

Consider a **high-availability database cluster** used in a global e-commerce platform. The system handles millions of transactions per day, with a large volume of product orders, customer data, and payment details.

To ensure uninterrupted service and optimal performance, the database cluster is designed with redundancy, load balancing, and automated maintenance.

Step 1: Database Cluster Design

The system is built using a **master-slave replication** architecture:

- The **master database** handles write operations.
- Multiple **replica (slave) databases** handle read operations, improving scalability.

Step 2: Regular Maintenance Tasks

- **Rebuilding Indexes**: Index fragmentation is monitored using the database's built-in tools. When fragmentation exceeds a threshold (e.g., 20%), indexes are rebuilt on the master database.

```sql
ALTER INDEX ALL ON orders REBUILD;
```

- **Vacuuming (PostgreSQL)**: The replica databases run VACUUM operations regularly to clean up dead rows and free up space.

```sql
VACUUM;
```

- **Archiving Old Data**: Historical sales data older than 1 year is archived to separate storage to keep the active database size manageable.

```sql
INSERT INTO archived_sales (SELECT * FROM sales WHERE sale_date < '2022-01-01');
DELETE FROM sales WHERE sale_date < '2022-01-01';
```

Step 3: Automating Backup and Recovery

Backups are automated using **AWS RDS** snapshots, and incremental backups are scheduled every 6 hours using **cron** jobs.

- Daily full backups are taken at midnight:

```bash
mysqldump -u username -p database_name |
gzip > /backups/database_name_$(date
+\%F).sql.gz
```

- Incremental backups are taken every 6 hours:

```bash
mysqldump -u username -p --incremental
database_name                          >
/backups/incremental_$(date +\%F_%H).sql
```

Step 4: Monitoring and Scaling

- **Monitoring**: The cluster is monitored using **Prometheus** and **Grafana** to keep track of CPU usage, disk space, and query performance. Alerts are set up for unusual spikes in load or slow-running queries.
- **Scaling**: As demand grows, additional replica nodes are added to the cluster to handle more read traffic. The

master node's capacity is also increased to handle write-heavy operations during peak times.

Conclusion

In this chapter, we explored essential **database maintenance** tasks to ensure that your SQL database remains healthy, performant, and scalable:

- **Indexing** and **vacuuming** help improve performance by reducing fragmentation and reclaiming space.
- **Managing database growth** through archiving, partitioning, and scaling is crucial for handling large datasets over time.
- We discussed how to **automate backups** and recovery in a **high-availability database cluster** to ensure minimal downtime and fast data recovery.

Regular maintenance is vital for keeping databases running efficiently and ensuring that they can handle the increasing demands of your applications. In the next chapter, we will focus on **database replication** and **high-availability configurations** to ensure your systems remain reliable and fault-tolerant.

CHAPTER 26

ADVANCED SQL TECHNIQUES: CTES, RECURSIVE QUERIES, AND WINDOW FUNCTIONS

As databases grow more complex, the need for advanced SQL techniques increases. In this chapter, we'll explore three essential advanced SQL techniques that can significantly enhance query performance and readability:

- **Common Table Expressions (CTEs)** for simplifying complex queries.
- **Recursive Queries** for handling hierarchical or recursive data structures.
- **Window Functions** for advanced analytics, including running totals and moving averages.

We will also walk through a **real-world example** of using **window functions** to build a running total of sales in a retail database.

1. Using Common Table Expressions (CTEs) for Readability

1.1. What is a Common Table Expression (CTE)?

A **Common Table Expression (CTE)** is a temporary result set that you can reference within a SELECT, INSERT, UPDATE, or DELETE statement. CTEs improve the readability and modularity of complex queries by breaking them into smaller, more manageable parts.

CTEs are particularly useful for:

- Breaking down long, complex queries.
- Avoiding the repetition of subqueries.
- Creating reusable, modular queries.

1.2. Syntax of CTEs

Here's the basic syntax for defining a CTE:

sql

```
WITH cte_name AS (
    -- Your query here
    SELECT column1, column2
    FROM table_name
    WHERE condition
)
SELECT column1, column2
FROM cte_name;
```

In this syntax:

- WITH introduces the CTE.
- cte_name is the name of the temporary result set.
- The query inside the parentheses defines the CTE.

1.3. Example of Using a CTE

Consider a query that retrieves the **top 5 products** based on sales from the orders table. Without a CTE, the query might look like this:

sql

```
SELECT product_id, SUM(quantity) AS total_sales
FROM orders
GROUP BY product_id
ORDER BY total_sales DESC
LIMIT 5;
```

Using a CTE, we can break down this query into two parts: one to calculate the total sales and another to retrieve the top 5 products.

sql

```
WITH sales_cte AS (
    SELECT    product_id,    SUM(quantity)    AS
total_sales
    FROM orders
```

293

```
    GROUP BY product_id
)
SELECT product_id, total_sales
FROM sales_cte
ORDER BY total_sales DESC
LIMIT 5;
```

In this example:

- The `sales_cte` CTE computes the total sales for each product.
- The main query then retrieves the top 5 products based on the `total_sales` from the CTE.

1.4. Benefits of Using CTEs

- **Readability**: CTEs make queries easier to read and maintain by organizing complex logic into smaller chunks.
- **Reusability**: You can reference the same CTE multiple times in your query, avoiding redundancy.

---

2. Writing Recursive Queries

2.1. What is a Recursive Query?

A **recursive query** is a query that refers to itself in order to retrieve hierarchical data. Recursive queries are useful for working with data that has a parent-child relationship, such as organizational hierarchies, file systems, or bill-of-materials structures.

A recursive query consists of two parts:

- **Base Case**: The first query in the recursive expression that returns the starting point (e.g., the root of a tree).
- **Recursive Case**: The query that repeatedly references the previous result to build up the complete hierarchy.

2.2. Syntax of Recursive Queries

Here's the basic syntax for a recursive query:

sql

```
WITH RECURSIVE cte_name AS (
    -- Base case: Select the root of the
hierarchy
    SELECT column1, column2
    FROM table_name
    WHERE condition
    UNION ALL
    -- Recursive case: Join the previous result
to the table to build the hierarchy
    SELECT t.column1, t.column2
    FROM table_name t
    JOIN cte_name cte
```

```
    ON t.parent_id = cte.column1
)
SELECT column1, column2
FROM cte_name;
```

- `WITH RECURSIVE` defines the recursive CTE.
- The base case selects the starting rows.
- The `UNION ALL` is used to combine the results of the recursive case with the base case.

2.3. Example of Recursive Query

Let's consider an **employee** table with a `manager_id` column, which refers to the `employee_id` of the manager. We want to retrieve all employees and their managers, up to the top-level manager.

sql

```
WITH RECURSIVE employee_hierarchy AS (
    -- Base case: Select the top-level manager
    SELECT          employee_id,          manager_id,
employee_name
    FROM employees
    WHERE manager_id IS NULL
    UNION ALL
    -- Recursive case: Select employees managed
by the previous result
```

296

```
    SELECT       e.employee_id,       e.manager_id,
e.employee_name
    FROM employees e
    JOIN employee_hierarchy eh ON e.manager_id =
eh.employee_id
)
SELECT * FROM employee_hierarchy;
```

In this query:

- The **base case** retrieves the top-level manager (where `manager_id` is `NULL`).
- The **recursive case** joins the `employees` table with the result of the previous query to retrieve employees managed by the previous set of employees.

This will return the entire employee hierarchy, starting from the top-level manager.

---

3. Understanding Window Functions for Running Totals and Analytics

3.1. What are Window Functions?

Window functions allow you to perform calculations across a set of rows related to the current row within the result set. Unlike aggregate functions (such as `SUM` or `AVG`), which operate on an entire group of rows, window functions can calculate values over a specific **window** of rows, without collapsing the result set.

Common use cases for window functions include:

- **Running totals**: Calculating the cumulative sum of a column.
- **Ranking**: Assigning a rank or row number to each row.
- **Moving averages**: Calculating averages over a rolling window.

3.2. Syntax of Window Functions

sql

```
SELECT column1, column2,
     WINDOW_FUNCTION()   OVER   (PARTITION   BY
column3 ORDER BY column4)
FROM table_name;
```

- **PARTITION BY** divides the result set into partitions to apply the window function on.
- **ORDER BY** determines the order of rows within each partition.

3.3. Example: Running Total of Sales

Let's say we have a `sales` table that records sales transactions, and we want to calculate a **running total** of sales.

298

sql

```
SELECT      transaction_id,      transaction_date,
total_amount,
        SUM(total_amount)    OVER     (ORDER    BY
transaction_date) AS running_total
FROM sales;
```

In this query:

- The SUM(total_amount) window function calculates the cumulative sum of total_amount.
- The ORDER BY transaction_date ensures that the running total is calculated in chronological order.

The result will show a running total of the sales amounts, with each row containing the total of all previous rows.

transaction_id	transaction_date	total_amount	running_total
1	2023-01-01	100.00	100.00
2	2023-01-02	200.00	300.00
3	2023-01-03	150.00	450.00
4	2023-01-04	50.00	500.00

3.4. Example: Ranking Products by Sales

You can also use window functions to assign rankings to rows based on a specific criterion. For example, let's rank products by their total sales:

sql

```
SELECT product_id, SUM(quantity) AS total_sales,
       RANK() OVER (ORDER BY SUM(quantity) DESC)
AS rank
FROM sales
GROUP BY product_id;
```

In this query:

- The `RANK()` function assigns a rank based on the total sales of each product.
- The `ORDER BY SUM(quantity) DESC` orders products by the total sales in descending order, so the product with the highest sales gets a rank of 1.

4. Real-World Example: Building a Running Total of Sales with Window Functions

Let's consider a **sales dashboard** where we want to display the total sales for each product, along with the running total of all sales up to that point.

Step 1: Define the `sales` Table

Assume we have a `sales` table with the following columns:

- `sale_id`: The ID of the sale.
- `product_id`: The ID of the product sold.
- `quantity`: The quantity of the product sold.
- `sale_date`: The date of the sale.

Step 2: Use Window Functions to Calculate the Running Total

We will use a window function to calculate the running total of sales for each product:

sql

```sql
SELECT product_id, sale_date, quantity,
       SUM(quantity)    OVER    (PARTITION    BY
product_id ORDER BY sale_date) AS running_total
FROM sales
ORDER BY product_id, sale_date;
```

This query calculates the running total for each product, ordered by `sale_date`, and partitions the data by `product_id`.

Conclusion

In this chapter, we explored several **advanced SQL techniques** to enhance query performance and improve data analysis capabilities:

- **Common Table Expressions (CTEs)**: Simplify complex queries and improve readability.
- **Recursive Queries**: Handle hierarchical or recursive data structures like organizational charts.
- **Window Functions**: Perform advanced analytics, such as running totals and ranking, over a specific window of rows.

We also worked through a **real-world example** of using **window functions** to calculate a running total of sales, providing powerful insights into your business data.

In the next chapter, we will explore **database security best practices** to ensure your SQL databases are secure and protected from unauthorized access and attacks.

CHAPTER 27

THE FUTURE OF SQL: TRENDS, TOOLS, AND BEYOND

As technology evolves, so does the way we interact with databases. **SQL** has been the cornerstone of relational database management systems (RDBMS) for decades, and while its fundamental principles remain largely unchanged, the landscape surrounding SQL is shifting in response to new challenges and innovations. The rise of **NoSQL**, **cloud databases**, and **real-time data processing** is reshaping how developers and data engineers use SQL to manage and manipulate data.

In this chapter, we will explore:

- **Trends in database technology** and SQL.
- The role of **SQL in the age of NoSQL** and **cloud databases**.
- How to **learn and adapt to new SQL tools and frameworks**.
- A **real-world example** of building **modern databases for real-time applications**.

1. Trends in Database Technology and SQL

1.1. SQL's Continued Relevance in Modern Applications

Despite the rise of **NoSQL** and alternative database technologies, **SQL** remains the most widely used language for interacting with relational databases. It is still the foundation of many business-critical applications, including financial systems, enterprise resource planning (ERP) systems, and customer relationship management (CRM) systems. As more organizations adopt **cloud computing** and **big data technologies**, SQL has evolved to meet the needs of modern applications.

Key trends that are shaping the future of SQL include:

- **Hybrid SQL/NoSQL Databases**: Many databases now support both SQL and NoSQL features. For instance, **PostgreSQL** has added support for **JSON** and **JSONB** data types, enabling developers to store and query structured and semi-structured data.

- **SQL on Big Data Platforms**: Platforms like **Google BigQuery**, **Amazon Redshift**, and **Apache Hive** allow SQL to be used for querying big data in distributed computing environments. These tools enable SQL developers to interact with large datasets, utilizing SQL's familiar syntax while benefiting from the scalability of big data systems.

1.2. Automation and AI in Database Management

Automation and artificial intelligence (AI) are transforming how databases are managed:

- **Automated Indexing and Query Optimization**: Modern database systems use machine learning algorithms to automatically optimize queries, create and drop indexes, and balance workloads without requiring manual intervention.
- **Database-as-a-Service (DBaaS)**: Cloud providers like **AWS**, **Azure**, and **Google Cloud** offer managed database services that handle scalability, security, and maintenance tasks, freeing developers to focus on their applications.
- **Self-Healing Databases**: Some newer databases are incorporating AI-driven systems for self-healing. These systems can automatically detect anomalies, diagnose issues, and apply fixes, making database administration more streamlined.

1.3. Real-Time Data Processing and Analytics

SQL is also making strides in handling **real-time data** and **analytics**:

- **Streaming SQL**: Tools like **Apache Kafka** and **Apache Flink** allow for real-time data streaming and processing. Streaming SQL extensions enable the use of SQL queries to process data in motion, making it possible to perform complex analytics on real-time data streams.

- **Real-Time Analytics**: SQL databases are increasingly incorporating real-time analytics capabilities, enabling businesses to make decisions based on up-to-the-minute data. Technologies like **SQL Server 2019's Big Data Clusters** and **Azure Synapse Analytics** support integration with big data and allow SQL-based queries on real-time data pipelines.

---

2. SQL in the Age of NoSQL and Cloud Databases

2.1. SQL vs. NoSQL: Complementary or Competitive?

While **NoSQL** databases like **MongoDB**, **Cassandra**, and **Couchbase** have gained popularity for their flexibility and scalability, SQL databases still offer significant advantages in scenarios where data integrity, relationships, and structured queries are important.

However, **NoSQL** databases excel in the following areas:

- **Schema flexibility**: NoSQL databases allow for schema-less or schema-flexible designs, making it easier to store unstructured or semi-structured data, such as documents, graphs, or key-value pairs.

- **Horizontal scalability**: NoSQL databases can scale horizontally by adding more nodes to the database cluster, making them a good fit for applications with large, distributed datasets.

Despite the rise of NoSQL, many modern applications use both SQL and NoSQL technologies in a **polyglot persistence** approach, choosing the right tool for the job. For example, a system might use **SQL** for transactional data and **NoSQL** for large-scale analytics or content storage.

2.2. The Rise of Cloud Databases

Cloud-based databases are becoming the go-to solution for businesses looking for flexible, scalable, and cost-effective database management. Cloud providers like **Amazon Web Services (AWS)**, **Microsoft Azure**, and **Google Cloud** offer a variety of SQL-based database services, such as **Amazon RDS**, **Azure SQL Database**, and **Cloud SQL**.

Benefits of cloud databases include:

- **Scalability**: Cloud databases offer easy horizontal scaling to accommodate growing data and traffic.
- **Managed Services**: Cloud providers handle backups, updates, security, and other administrative tasks, reducing the operational burden on developers.

- **Global Availability**: With cloud databases, data can be replicated across different regions, ensuring low latency and high availability.

2.3. SQL as a Service

Cloud providers also offer **Database-as-a-Service (DBaaS)**, which allows organizations to offload database management and focus on application development:

- **Fully Managed SQL Databases**: Services like **Amazon RDS**, **Azure SQL Database**, and **Google Cloud SQL** handle database provisioning, backups, patching, and scaling without requiring in-depth database administration skills.
- **Serverless Databases**: Serverless offerings like **AWS Aurora Serverless** and **Azure SQL Database serverless** automatically scale compute resources based on demand, making it easy to handle fluctuating workloads while minimizing costs.

3. Learning and Adapting to New SQL Tools and Frameworks

3.1. Embracing New SQL Extensions and Frameworks

SQL developers must adapt to new tools and frameworks that enhance their capabilities. Some notable extensions and frameworks include:

- **SQL-on-Hadoop**: Tools like **Apache Hive**, **Presto**, and **Apache Impala** allow you to run SQL queries on big data platforms like **Hadoop** and **Spark**.
- **Graph Databases**: SQL extensions for graph data, like **SQL/PGQ** for **PostgreSQL** or **SQL Server's graph capabilities**, allow developers to work with graph data models for use cases such as social networks, fraud detection, and recommendation engines.
- **NoSQL Interfaces**: Some relational databases, such as **PostgreSQL** and **MySQL**, now offer NoSQL-like features (e.g., JSON support), allowing developers to use SQL alongside NoSQL data structures.

3.2. Staying Up-to-Date with SQL Innovations

SQL is not static—new innovations are constantly being added to improve performance, scalability, and ease of use. As a developer, it's important to stay informed about:

- **SQL Standard Updates**: Keep an eye on updates to the SQL standard (e.g., **SQL:2016**), which introduces new features and improvements.

- **Cloud SQL Tools**: Familiarize yourself with cloud-based tools and services, such as **BigQuery**, **Redshift**, and **Snowflake**, which provide highly scalable, fully managed SQL databases with specialized capabilities for cloud environments.

- **Advanced Analytics and AI in SQL**: Look for opportunities to leverage SQL in conjunction with machine learning and artificial intelligence for predictive analytics, anomaly detection, and other advanced use cases.

---

4. Real-World Example: Building Modern Databases for Real-Time Applications

Consider a **real-time application** used by a global financial services company. The system needs to process large volumes of transactional data in real-time to provide up-to-the-minute stock market prices, account balances, and transaction history.

Step 1: Using SQL for Real-Time Data Processing

The company utilizes **PostgreSQL** to store transactional data, such as user account balances and stock trades. To support real-time analytics, they implement **window functions** to calculate running totals for account balances and daily profits.

```sql
sql

SELECT account_id, transaction_date, amount,
       SUM(amount) OVER (PARTITION BY account_id
ORDER BY transaction_date) AS running_balance
FROM transactions
WHERE transaction_date BETWEEN '2023-01-01' AND
'2023-12-31';
```

Step 2: Implementing a Hybrid SQL/NoSQL Architecture

While PostgreSQL is used for structured transaction data, the system also uses **MongoDB** for storing unstructured data such as user preferences and stock price history. The two databases are integrated using **Apache Kafka**, allowing real-time data to flow between systems.

Step 3: Scaling and Optimizing the Database

The system is hosted on **AWS** using **RDS for PostgreSQL** for the SQL database and **Elasticache** for caching frequently queried data. **AWS Aurora** handles the high availability and scalability requirements. The company leverages **serverless database scaling** to dynamically adjust compute resources based on transaction volume, ensuring optimal performance during peak times.

Conclusion

In this chapter, we explored the future of SQL and how it is evolving in response to new trends and technologies:

- **SQL continues to be relevant** in the age of NoSQL and cloud databases, with innovations like hybrid databases and SQL-on-Hadoop platforms extending its capabilities.
- **Cloud databases** and **DBaaS** are making database management easier and more scalable.
- Learning new SQL tools, frameworks, and extensions will help developers stay competitive in a rapidly changing environment.

We also discussed a **real-world example** of building modern databases for a real-time application, demonstrating the use of SQL alongside NoSQL tools and cloud technologies.

In the next chapter, we will dive deeper into **SQL performance tuning**, exploring advanced optimization techniques for large-scale systems.

www.ingramcontent.com/pod-product-compliance
Lightning Source LLC
LaVergne TN
LVHW051433050326
832903LV00030BD/3056